Interview to
Succeed

Insider Secrets for Landing the Job

R.J. Bindner

iUniverse LLC
Bloomington

INTERVIEW TO SUCCEED
INSIDER SECRETS FOR LANDING THE JOB

iUniverse books may be ordered through booksellers or by contacting:

iUniverse
1663 Liberty Drive
Bloomington, IN 47403
www.iuniverse.com
1-800-Authors (1-800-288-4677)

For information contact:

The R.J. Bindner Group, LLC
118 N. Peters Road
Suite 175
Knoxville, TN 37923

ISBN: 978-1-4917-1101-9 (sc)
ISBN: 978-1-4917-1102-6 (e)

Printed in the United States of America.

iUniverse rev. date: 3/10/2014

Dedicated to those who press on.

Contents

Introduction

I wrote this book with one purpose in mind: to help people win the job competition. We all tend to believe the most qualified candidate will be selected for a given opportunity. However, "most qualified" is a soft concept.

In the minds of hiring managers, there are many attributes that make up the "most qualified" candidate. One candidate may have perfect grades, belong to all the right clubs, and appear to be an obvious choice. However, another candidate may have great leadership or work experience, good interpersonal skills, and the ability to better demonstrate why he is the best choice.

The winner of any job competition will be the candidate who is best able to sell his qualifications and is the best fit with the hiring manager's organization. Yes, I said *sell* his qualifications. Your entire purpose in a job interview is to sell yourself—to educate the hiring manager on your incredible skill set and the great contributions you will make to the organization. Thus, the key to success in a job competition is the ability to master the interview process and sell yourself better than any other candidate in the interview pool.

Unfortunately, many job candidates fail to understand the importance of conveying their key skills and attributes to hiring managers in the interview process. According to the University of Tennessee Career Services Department's interviewing guide for students (http://career.utk.edu/CS/wp-content/uploads/pdf/Job-Interview.pdf) "Here in UT Career Services we have a long standing tradition of surveying on-campus recruiters to gauge how well students do while being interviewed for position openings. Like clockwork each year employers rate UT students low in two areas 1) *"Knowledge of how to sell themselves to the employer"* and 2) *"Students had researched our organization"*.

One of the most important aspects of your job search is preparation for the interview process. There are many interview models used by hiring managers in today's job environment. Some of the more common models are:

- situational
- case
- stress
- behavior-based

The first three interview models are based primarily on hypothetical information. In the *situational model*, the hiring manager will ask candidates how they would respond or react to various scenarios or situations. For example, the manager might say, "Tell me how you would deal with a coworker who was not doing his fair share of the work." In the *case model*, the hiring manager might outline a situation, problem, or case study and ask you to formulate a plan or discuss how you would solve the problem. In the *stress model*, hiring managers ask similarly open-ended questions, but they also apply stressors to unnerve you—responding to your answer with sarcasm, for example, or sitting quietly after you've responded to assess how you behave in an uncomfortable situation.

These common models deal in the hypothetical and fail to adequately assess a candidate's possession of the desired competencies for a given position. However, the *behavior-based model* deeply examines a candidate's past behaviors to make a link between a candidate's demonstrated competencies and an organization's desired competencies. According to career expert and author Dr. Katharine Hansen, behavioral interviewing is 55 percent predictive of future on-the-job behavior, while traditional interviewing is only 10 percent predictive. This book will provide you with deep insight into what is arguably the most effective and dynamic interview model used by hiring managers today: the behavior-based interview model or BBI.

The development of the BBI model is generally credited to Dr. Paul Green of Behavioral Technology, Inc. The company trademarked the name Behavioral Interviewing and defined it as an analysis of a candidate's potential abilities by examining skills that have been used in past job performance. Dr. Green is said to have coined the phrase, "Past behavior is the best predictor of future performance." The BBI model is such a detailed, effective model,

I believe it should be used as preparation by anyone planning to go out for interviews. Even if a different model is used during the actual interview, the BBI model will prepare you well enough to adapt and excel.

Preparation is critical, and you have already leapt far ahead of your competition simply by choosing this book. I have spent years employing the BBI model as a hiring manager and on hiring teams in the biotech pharmaceutical industry. In this book, I will walk you through the BBI model and offer guidance as you prepare for your interview. I will provide you with real-world insight and keys to success based on my experience.

I have reviewed countless resumes over the years and will share with you firsthand the types of resumes that catch my attention. I will share examples of the structure and content of cover and thank-you letters that make an impact. I will provide you with 125 actual interview questions. I will walk you through a typical interview process from start to finish, provide insight, and prepare you to excel.

The power to win the job of your dreams is in your hands. Absorb the insights provided throughout this book and work hard to prepare your interview presentation. Then rehearse your presentation to near perfection. All the effort invested in preparation will pay off in the form of confidence and success during the interview process.

1   Understanding the Interview Process

Understanding the full interview process is a critical step in preparing for success. We all have similar questions when facing these situations: What are they looking for? What is the recruitment process? What is the next step after they respond to my application? How should I prepare for the interview?

There is much more to the interview process than the interview itself. By knowing the process, you will understand how the company and the hiring manager have prepared, where you stand, and what lies ahead. Knowing these things will not only preserve your sanity, it will provide you with valuable insight as you prepare for the next step.

The process I will be describing is a very general one. The specifics will vary among organizations, but the core elements tend to be very similar. In this chapter, we will focus on the following phases of the interview process:

1. Job design and competency development
2. Recruiting strategy development
3. Screening
4. Face-to-face interview
5. Job offer
6. Pre-employment

Most organizations form hiring teams to fill open positions. The hiring manager will make the final decision on which candidate to hire. However, the team approach allows the manager to elicit numerous opinions on a given candidate. Hiring teams may consist of the hiring manager, other managers and employees within the organization, and human resources (HR).

In most organizations, HR conducts the first three phases of the process. In fact, the department plays a critical role in the hiring process from beginning to end. Much of its work is completed in advance of the initiation of the hiring process and is conducted primarily behind the scenes. HR is responsible for *job design* and *competency development,* which includes writing the job description and identifying the skills—the competencies—that prospective candidates must possess to be successful in this particular organization. The development of these competencies is not done in a vacuum. HR consults with various areas of the company, such as management and training, to gain input into this critical element of the process.

As you prepare for the interview process, your primary focus should be on job competencies. For reasons that will become clear as you continue through this book, your entire presentation will be centered on these competencies. I will provide very in-depth details surrounding this topic and will guide you in building your interview presentation.

HR also develops the company's *recruiting strategy.* The department has numerous options available for recruiting prospective candidates. Following are three of the most common recruiting methods available to HR:

1. Search the company database for suitable candidates.
2. Post jobs on the company website and in the media.
3. Hire agencies to recruit candidates.

Searching the company database for resumes that have been submitted by candidates in the past is not something that companies often do, in my experience. As new job openings arise, previously submitted resumes tend to be viewed as stale, and a new recruiting process is initiated to net fresh candidates. Don't assume that because your resume is "on file," you will automatically be considered for any openings.

Posting job openings on the corporate website yields few candidates, because only those who actively monitor the site will see the posting. However, the few candidates who surface through this route will likely have a high level of interest in the organization. Virtually all companies post job openings on their corporate website as a formality, but it is seldom the sole strategy employed.

A popular recruiting strategy that yields a high volume of candidates is posting job openings with media outlets like job boards. The results are the opposite of the company website strategy: while the volume of applicants is high, many may be unqualified or know little about the organization.

Probably the most common recruiting method used by large companies is external recruiting agencies that specialize in specific industries or functions. Companies generally use recruiting agencies with which they have worked in the past and have developed a degree of trust. Hiring managers tend to rely on them to find the highest-quality candidates.

Recruiting agencies are notified of the type of candidate a hiring manager is seeking, and they attempt to provide as many qualified candidates as possible. These agencies are compensated by the client company if one of their candidates is hired. Therefore, it is in a recruiting agency's best interest to provide a large number of qualified candidates and to sell each candidate's merits to the hiring manager.

Recruiting agencies typically do not provide much, if any, assistance in the form of interview preparation or resume writing. What they do provide is a relationship with their client companies and managers that can fast-track your resume directly to the hiring manager. These recruiting agencies represent the best opportunity for a candidate to get a foot in the door of a given organization or industry.

You can easily find recruiting agencies by searching "recruiters" on the Internet for your industry or function. I recommend that you identify two or three recruiting agencies with which you feel comfortable and work with them exclusively. Many recruiters work in networks that allow all network recruiters to view the same opportunities. Working with too many recruiters can result in a duplication of efforts and waste valuable time for both the agency and the candidate. A few key considerations when selecting agencies are industry focus, experience, success rates in placing candidates, and the quality of the companies they represent.

The process to this point is focused on providing the hiring manager with the most qualified candidates to move into the interview phase. With the exception of their potential involvement in the phone-screening process, your interaction with HR will be minimal until you reach the job offer phase.

After the administrative functions related to the job design have been completed and the recruiting strategy has been implemented, the hiring manager will typically be presented with a portfolio of resumes. The resumes represent a hiring manager's first opportunity to explore his candidates. At this point, it will suffice for you to know that hiring managers look for specific items on resumes, and this phase represents the first round of cuts from the manager's candidate pool.

Upon completion of the resume review, the hiring manager should have a pool of well-qualified candidates to move forward in the process. Your first goal is to make it into this pool of candidates. If you are successful, that means you're viewed by the company as a candidate who potentially possesses the competencies required for success in the organization. However, this is just a preliminary judgment based on your resume. I will discuss developing a resume that gets you to this point in chapter 4.

The next step, at most companies, is *screening*. The purpose of the screening phase is to ascertain whether you truly possess the qualities conveyed in your resume. Most companies use the phone screen as their initial screening tool. Hiring managers conduct these screenings in many cases. It is their first opportunity to hold a live discussion with a candidate, develop an initial impression, and determine whether they want to move the candidate forward in the process. However, some managers and companies prefer to have an HR specialist conduct the phone screen and determine who to move forward.

The typical phone screen lasts between thirty and sixty minutes, but there is no time limit. The goals of the phone screen are similar to the more in-depth face-to-face interview and include, but are not limited to, the following:

- Assess the candidate's communication skills.
- Measure the candidate's knowledge of the company and industry.
- Determine why a candidate wants to work for this company.
- Ascertain what a candidate has to offer.
- Measure the candidate's understanding of the job.
- Measure the candidate's familiarity with the required job competencies.
- Judge how the candidate's past performance has demonstrated the required competencies.
- Assess the candidate's level of passion and motivation.

The key to successfully passing a phone screen is preparation. We will discuss this topic in more depth in chapter 6, where I will highlight some simple strategies for success in this phase of the process.

As you are beginning to see, there is far more to the interview process than conducting an interview. Following the screening phase, the hiring manager will identify the best candidates and move them into the *face-to-face interview* phase. In this phase, candidates will typically participate in a minimum of three interviews.

The first interview will be with the hiring manager. This is the manager's first opportunity to sit face-to-face with the group of candidates she has selected. The first interview is designed to identify the strongest candidates and weed out those less qualified. The hiring manager is looking for any reason to narrow her pool of candidates, including poor eye contact, poor grammar, lack of preparation, and weak presentation skills. Candidates at this stage must be at their best.

The second interview, for selected candidates, will typically be with the hiring manager's boss. The hiring manager's boss does not typically make hiring decisions. Hiring managers send candidates to interview with their bosses in order to get a second, more experienced opinion on the candidate's "fit" for the position. Following the interviews, the two managers will meet to discuss the candidates.

The third interview is typically a revisit with the hiring manager. Many managers will make a hiring decision after the second round of face-to-face interviews, but some may choose to conduct this third round. They may want to meet with final candidates again to confirm their initial thoughts or to further assess a targeted skill set, such as presentation skills.

Following these three rounds of face-to-face interviews, it is possible that a hiring manager will move to the job offer phase of the process. However, if she is uncertain, she has other options before deciding on a candidate. For example, she may have the final candidates interview with another manager or spend a day on the job with one of her veteran employees. These options allow the hiring manager to elicit additional insight before making her final decision as to whom she will offer the position.

The next step in the process depends on a candidate's level of success. HR will contact unsuccessful candidates to thank them for their interest and notify them that the hiring manager has decided against their candidacy. Successful candidates will move into the *job offer* phase.

The job offer will usually not occur during the final interview. For legal and regulatory reasons, a great deal of time and effort are put into developing an offer for a candidate. The hiring manager may give her preferred candidate some indication in the final interview that an offer is pending. However, that is not always the case. Another benefit of working with a recruiting agency is that the agency works closely with the hiring company through the entire process. They will be able to provide you with updates and let you know where you stand.

Ultimately, the chosen candidate will receive a phone call from the hiring organization, and the offer will be presented. The timeline from the conclusion of the final interview to the telephone call presenting the offer will vary, but is generally anywhere from one day to one week.

Following a candidate's acceptance of a company's offer, a few final steps remain in the *pre-employment* phase before a candidate becomes an employee at most organizations. The candidate will be given a tentative start date and an offer letter contingent on acceptable reference and background checks. Some employers may also require drug screening and a physical examination. Combined, these final measures might take a few days to a week to complete.

Do not let the complexity of the interview process discourage you. Although it sounds endless, the full process typically lasts from one to four weeks on average. Regardless of the process, you have three responsibilities:

1. Prepare an effective resume to get a phone screen.
2. Perform effectively in a phone screen to get a face-to-face interview.
3. Perform effectively in a face-to-face interview to get a job offer.

Take advantage of the information provided in this book to learn what hiring managers are seeking, and you will be light-years ahead of your competition. Remember, it will all be worth it in the end when the job is yours.

2 | Learning the Behavior-Based Interview Model

Now that you have an understanding of the interview process and the various phases through which you must progress successfully to win the job of your dreams, we will examine the BBI model. It is one of the most common and most effective interview models in which hiring managers are trained to interview candidates and identify talent.

In this chapter, I will explain the model in detail, give guidance on how to identify what the hiring manager is seeking in a candidate, and help you begin to understand how you can exceed those expectations. Once you understand how hiring managers are trained and what they seek, you will be ready to develop your interview strategy.

Remember, although some general guidance may be provided in this chapter, it is primarily focused on explaining the interview process from the hiring manager's perspective. I will focus on *your* actions and strategies as they relate to this model after you have developed an understanding of what hiring managers are seeking in candidates.

Different companies may refer to the BBI model by different names, such as *targeted selection* or *competency interviewing*, but the concept is the same. BBI is simply a technique for examining a person's past behaviors to determine if he or she has exhibited the competencies required to perform a job. History and experience show that there is no better predictor of future success than past performance. If a person has excelled in multiple jobs and capacities in the past, it is a good indicator of the quality of that person. It is unlikely that a high performer is going to wake up one day and decide to become a low performer.

The BBI model is designed to allow managers to take a walk down memory lane and review a candidate's past. They are seeking a track record of success and details on how you were able to achieve it. They are trained to develop questions to dig deep into your background to understand your thought process. Was your success a fluke? Was it luck? Or was it the result of focused, well-planned hard work and strong skills?

Consider the following question: "Tell me about a time you operated as part of a team and achieved a significant success." This is not a hypothetical question. The BBI model teaches hiring managers to focus on achievements and continue to peel back layers to get to the behaviors that contributed to the success. The hiring manager will expect specific details about your actions and involvement in the success. Numerous follow-up questions will target the details of your actions in an attempt to identify whether you have displayed the competencies the manager is seeking.

In a traditional interview, a candidate may tell a great story about how he or she achieved success. For example, one candidate was asked the following question: "Can you tell me about one of your greatest accomplishments and how you achieved it?" His initial answer sounded great:

> I was able to gain access into an office of eight "no see" customers, including some of the industry's top buyers. That allowed me to grow my market share to number two in the nation.

In other interview models, that answer would be sufficient, and the interviewer would go on to the next question. However, hiring managers trained in BBI will dig deeper to get to the root behavior. Follow-up questions to that answer will be similar to these:

- How were you able to gain access to the office?
- Who helped you in the office?
- How did you identify who to go to for help?
- How did you persuade that individual to help you?
- Once in the office, which buyers did you target?
- Why did you target that buyer?
- How did you determine which buyers to target?
- What actions did you take to build the relationship?

This technique achieves many objectives, including determining the true level of knowledge and involvement of a candidate. If a candidate had minimal involvement in a success or is exaggerating a success, that will become apparent under intense scrutiny. A high level of discomfort can lead an unprepared candidate to squirm in an interview.

There is a bright side to this, however. Your knowledge of the BBI model, coupled with intense preparation, can lead you to shine in such an interview. You need to go deep in your preparation. Think through your examples and stories in detail. Hiring managers want plentiful details and examples to allow them to analyze how you think. They want to determine whether your actions match the required competencies they deem important to success in their organization. Though it's hard on those who walk in unprepared, this BBI process does, by design, enable the well-prepared candidate to excel. By following the guidance in this book, you will be prepared, confident, and poised for success.

Keep in mind, no hiring manager wishes to breach the confidentiality of another organization. The direct line of questioning is intended to elicit detailed examples of *your* skills and behaviors, not confidential information. If at any time you feel that a response to an interview question involves proprietary or confidential information, simply inform the hiring manager of your dilemma and refrain from providing that information.

There are two specific components of the BBI model:

1. Job design and competency identification
2. Behavior-based interview execution

As we discuss each component in depth, you will gain an understanding of what is expected of a successful candidate. Also, possibly for the first time, you will develop a strategic mental picture of how to prepare for an interview, structure responses to interview questions, and design your interview strategy. Your deeper understanding will be refined in later chapters as we discuss your interview preparation in more detail.

Job Design and Competency Identification

One of a manager's first steps in the hiring process is reviewing the job design and identifying required competencies for a given position. Unless it is a newly created position, HR will have completed these two tasks long before.

Job design typically refers to the scope of responsibility within the job—what employees are expected to do in this position. For example:

- Develop and maintain key customer relationships.
- Develop customer solutions that result in increased sales volume.

Competencies are the skills necessary, or desired, for a candidate to be successful in the position. Below is a list of common competencies:

- motivating others
- teamwork
- business acumen
- resource-planning skills
- critical-thinking skills
- relationship building and networking
- fostering mutual trust and respect
- written and spoken communication
- organization skills
- company/market/industry knowledge
- product knowledge
- computer skills
- analytical skills
- strategic planning
- creativity
- self-motivation
- striving for continual development

Once the hiring manager has identified the required competencies, he is ready to begin his interview preparation. Managers will use their competency list to develop their list of initial questions for candidates. Their questions will be designed to elicit examples of past behaviors that illustrate a candidate's possession of the desired competencies.

For example, if a manager is assessing your persuasion or communication skills, he might ask a question like, "Tell me about a time you had to sell your boss on an idea he disliked." Most managers will have a list of favorite BBI questions and will apply those questions to all candidates. Posing a similar set of questions to all candidates gives a manager an equal standard by which to measure them.

Behavior-Based Interview Execution

This section contains some of the most important information on BBI as it pertains to your quest to earn your desired position. In this section, we will discuss the four elements of behavioral information and the STAR format that is expected for your responses.

The four elements of behavioral information

The BBI process trains hiring managers to evaluate answers based on the following four types of behavioral information:

1. Demonstrable
2. Detailed
3. Verifiable/quantifiable
4. Historical

As we have discussed, strong answers will be tied to examples of how candidates have demonstrated desired behaviors that illustrate possession of the job competencies.

The key word in the previous sentence is *demonstrated*. Answers that discuss how "focused" you were on project completion or the fact that you were the "best" designer on your team are abstract. They are not behaviors that can be demonstrated. However, "I recorded and analyzed detailed notes for future planning purposes" provides an example of behaviors that led to your success. These behaviors may demonstrate that you are focused on your job or that you go the extra mile to create a "record" and "analyze" it to identify greater opportunities. The following table provides examples of demonstrable behaviors versus nondemonstrable behaviors to further clarify this concept.

Nondemonstrable Behaviors	Demonstrable Behaviors
I was the most analytical person on my team.	I developed sales-analysis reports that were adopted by my manager for the full team.
I was the best sales representative on my team.	I developed [sales tactic x], which led to the highest sales growth on my team.
I was the hardest worker on my team.	I exceeded the national sales-call average every month during my tenure.
I was the most strategic person on my team.	I recorded notes after each meeting and analyzed them to identify business opportunities.
I had the best business relationships on my team.	I conducted weekly dinners with my top three customers and received a customer-service award.

Hiring managers will also expect very *detailed* answers. To effectively evaluate your past behaviors and how they correlate with the preferred job competencies, hiring managers will seek as many details as possible. Consider the question, "Tell me about a time you played a role in a team success." A typical response might be:

> I worked with my medical liaison and created a new presentation for use at Medicaid meetings, and it was adopted by the organization for national use.

However, a more effective answer would include your identification and analysis of the problem, the team you built to develop possible solutions, the process by which you identified the most effective option, steps you took to implement the solution, and the results of your efforts. Again, think through your stories from start to finish and provide all relevant details when conveying the story.

Your answers should always be *verifiable*. Candidates can, and do, make all sorts of claims in interviews. Hiring managers are aware of the propensity for some to exaggerate and will measure claims based on your ability to support them. If you claim to be the number-one ranked sales professional on your team, the hiring manager will expect to see documentation supporting that claim. If you cannot produce supporting documentation, your claim will carry no weight. All of your claims should be verifiable. We will discuss the construction of a presentation binder, or brag book, in chapter 3 to help you with this component.

Hiring managers also have a strong affinity for *quantifiable* information—that is, information that can be measured. Growth percentages, market-share changes, project success rates, and any other form of measureable information allows a hiring manager to evaluate your past performance with a much higher degree of precision. If the national-average market share for a given product is 10 percent but you have achieved a 20 percent market share in your territory, there is no disputing the fact that you have effectively outperformed the nation. Quantifiable results from previous positions or endeavors offer one of your best opportunities to make a strong impression.

You should speak to any and all accomplishments you have achieved in the past. However, you must refrain from embellishing your stories. Remember, one of the strengths of the BBI model is the ability to uncover exaggerations. A skilled interviewer can easily uncover inaccuracies in a candidate's story. In addition to skillful, detailed questioning, hiring managers are typically trained in evaluating nonverbal behavior. If you begin squirming as the interviewer hones in on the details of a story you have embellished, the interviewer will notice that. His training will lead him to focus on the cause of your discomfort to draw out more details. The bottom line is, you have too much to lose over an exaggeration.

Finally, your examples should be *historical*. References or claims related to the future are hypothetical. The focus of BBI is to examine your past behaviors to determine whether you have exhibited the desired competencies in previous positions, not imagine what you might theoretically do in the future.

The STAR format

As a strong candidate, you are probably beginning to formulate answers and questions in your mind. Let me provide you with some structure to start you down the right path. All of your answers to interview questions should be structured as follows:

1. **S**ituation or **T**ask: What was the situation or circumstances of the event?

2. **A**ction: What did you do in response? What actions did you take?
3. **R**esult: What results did your actions produce?

Talk through your stories and responses from start to finish when formulating them for potential interview questions. Be able to discuss why you made every decision and how you made the decision. Consider the question, "Where did you attend college and why?" I have heard people respond to this question with, "I attended [College X] because that is where I got accepted." Remember, you are trying to demonstrate that you are decisive, driven, and goal-oriented. A strong answer would include concrete reasons for targeting your particular college, the detailed process you engaged in to make the decision to attend that college, the process you implemented to ensure acceptance, and how well you did in your studies and extracurricular activities.

As you continue through this chapter, begin to train your mind to respond in this appropriate manner. Stories and past successes will likely begin entering your mind. Practice formulating these stories and successes in the STAR format. Make notes of them as you go so you can remember and refine them at a later time.

The STAR format is how hiring managers expect, or at least would like, to receive answers to their questions. Based on my hiring experience, candidates rarely provide answers in this manner—but they definitely get my attention when they do. With preparation and practice, you will greatly impress any hiring manager with this technique. However, the STAR format only provides the desired structure for your answer. Remember that hiring managers are also evaluating the content of your answers.

In summary, when preparing answers to potential interview questions, think them through from start to finish. Convey as many relevant details as possible. Provide examples of your behavior that are demonstrable, detailed, verifiable/quantifiable, and historical. Finally, structure your answers using the STAR format.

Now that you are armed with the knowledge of how you will be evaluated in a behavior-based interview, continue through this book to master the art of excelling within this system. Learn how to build the stories of your accomplishments around the job competencies and masterfully respond to an interviewer's questions, and you will have companies fighting to hire you.

3 | Preparing for the Interview of Your Life

A job search is a highly competitive endeavor. You can be certain that the other job candidates, your competition, are of the highest caliber. However, regardless of their education or work experience, the ability to interview well is what matters most.

Remember, in the eyes of the hiring manager, there is no area where you are more knowledgeable than your own personal history. If you cannot present yourself well and sell yourself in an interview, you may never successfully earn the position you desire. Therefore, in-depth knowledge, understanding, and pure mastery of the interview process will greatly enhance your potential for success in the interview competition.

In this chapter, we will begin to develop the tools you will use in your interview presentation. I refer to the interview as a "presentation" because that is exactly what you are doing. The entire process is a presentation of you, your past performance, and the indicators of your future performance.

To conduct an effective presentation, you need the right tools. We will begin by developing and refining responses to interview questions that support the competencies of the job for which you are interviewing. We will also discuss preparing a "brag book" or presentation binder to help verify and quantify the details of your accomplishments. Another important, but often poorly devised, tool is the business plan. We will discuss an effective format for this tool and its use in the interview. Time will also be spent discussing the importance of company and industry research. Finally, the importance of the "Why Me" page will be discussed.

Once you have developed these important tools of the trade, you will be prepared to put it all together and begin work on the actual execution of the interview. It is worth noting that these tools need only be developed once, not over and over again for every interview. Some details will need to be modified or updated based on the company, position, competencies, etc. However, the primary effort in developing the tools should only occur once.

Developing Answers to Support Competencies

We will take very specific steps to ensure that your catalog of success stories is adequately developed and that it supports the job competencies desired by the hiring manager. To accomplish this, focus on the following:

1. Identify job competencies for the position.
2. Develop your catalog of story lines and examples.
3. Practice with sample questions and develop responses.
4. Begin tying your responses to the job competencies.

The first step in your preparation is to *identify desired skills*, or competencies, for the company with which you are interviewing. This should be a simple procedure and require minimal time.

You will have several options for discovering these competencies. Perhaps the simplest route is to go to the website for the company with which you are interviewing. Go to the "careers" section and identify the position for which you are applying. Typically, companies will list the required competencies with the job description.

However, should your targeted company not have them listed, you have other options. If you are working with a recruiting agency, your recruiter should be able to provide the competencies. If you are working directly with the HR department of a company, simply request the job competencies from your HR contact.

The second step is to *begin building your story lines and examples*. I recommend you begin by listing your achievements, failures, experiences, skills, strengths, weaknesses, and character traits. Next, identify the factors that contributed to your achievements and failures, as well as what you learned from them. For example, did you succeed or fail because of certain skills or because of a particular character trait?

Think through meaningful experiences in which you learned new skills or lessons. This could involve previous work experience, college experiences, clubs, teams, or any environment in which you added to your skill set. Maybe you developed leadership skills on a sports team or learned computer skills at a previous job. Identify all of your skills. Think of all the things you have learned to do and things you are good at doing. Conduct a self-analysis and list your strengths and weaknesses.

Finally, list your character traits. Are you tenacious and someone who refuses to quit? Are you compassionate, with a desire to help people? As you begin developing responses to the plethora of interview questions you will hear, all of these things have the potential to be part of your story line.

Once you have developed your initial story lines and examples, I recommend you go to the list of sample interview questions in chapter 7 and *practice answering questions*. As you do, a few things will occur. First, you will refine your initial story lines and examples. Second, you will expand your thoughts. Story lines and examples that have long been forgotten will come rushing back. You will generate new ideas on how to present and apply your examples. The more you practice answering questions, the better you will get at answering them.

There's an art to presenting your personal traits and performance history. You want every aspect of your interview presentation to be refined, impactful, and as near perfect as possible. Candidates who fail to prepare adequately respond with lackluster answers; they stutter, stammer, and fail to impress. With adequate preparation, your answers will be well thought-out. The content will be complete, and you will be able to discuss them in a clear, succinct, and professional manner.

Consider the common open-ended question "Tell me about yourself." Candidates commonly provide a thirty-second response that sounds similar to this:

> I grew up in a small town outside of Tampa. I graduated from high school in 2009 and moved to Gainesville to attend the University of Florida. I graduated in 2013 with a degree in business management, and now I'm here interviewing with you.

A more refined, impressive response might sound similar to this:

I grew up outside of Tampa and graduated from high school in 2009. I had two primary criteria when selecting a college. First, I needed to stay in state for the purpose of tuition. Second, I wanted to attend a school with a strong business program [*situation/task*].

I spent six months during my junior year researching business programs in the state of Florida. My research was focused on three areas: the quality of the incoming students based on national test scores and grade point averages, the quality of the program based on national rankings, and the number of nationally recognized professors. Based on those criteria, I identified the University of Florida as the best option [*action*].

While attending the university, I was a four-year varsity track runner, vice president of the college basket weavers club for two years, and president of my sorority for two years. I graduated in 2013 with a degree in business management and a 3.74 grade point average. My career interests lie within the financial sector, and that is what led me to you. This is a great opportunity with an industry leader, and I am very excited about discussing the contributions I can make to your organization [*result*].

While practicing your answers to the sample questions, remember you play the way you practice. Your answers need to convey as many relevant details as possible. Ensure that your answers provide examples of your behavior that are demonstrable, detailed, verifiable/quantifiable, and historical. Finally, structure your answer using the STAR format (situation/task, action, results) where appropriate.

After you have spent ample time rehearsing answers and have developed a strong catalog of story lines, it is time to begin *tying them into job competencies*. You will find, if your preparation has been done effectively, that you have developed multiple answers for any question related to a given competency. I recommend you sit down with the list of job competencies and spend time creating responses that illustrate the fact that you possess the desired competency.

For example, if a company has "creativity" listed as a job competency, you might have a story about the unique solution you developed to solve a problem at work or a creative campaign strategy that got you elected to a student-body office. As we will discuss in chapter 6, a key interview strategy will be to highlight the job competencies and then discuss how you have demonstrated those competencies in previous positions.

Showcasing Your Qualifications with a Brag Book

The purpose of a brag book is twofold. First, it provides a way for you to verify your performance claims. Second, it facilitates your presentation of your past achievements. Arriving for an interview without a brag book can be a costly mistake. When interviewing for open positions, I routinely rule out candidates who fail to bring documentation to support their performance claims. As discussed previously, one of the goals of the initial round of interviews is to rule candidates out. You have to be at the top of your game to progress in the interview process, and the brag book is a necessary tool to accomplish this.

Every candidate's brag book is different. Books vary from a few pages listing awards to binders so full of information that an interviewer could never read it all. I recommend preparing two different brag books:

1. An abbreviated version to be mailed to the interview team
2. A complete version for your use during the interview

Mailing an abbreviated brag book gives you a leg up on your competition by demonstrating initiative. It also provides the hiring manager with time to increase his knowledge and comfort level with your candidacy prior to the interview. I recommend mailing a brag book to every person with whom you will interview.

With the mailed brag book, your goal is to simply provide the highlights of your candidacy. I recommend a small binder that includes your resume, cover letter, last evaluation, awards, and anything you feel is critical for the hiring manager to see. For example, if you are interviewing for a position in the financial services industry and you have a certificate for outstanding contributions during a financial services internship, I would include it.

The brag book for use during your interview should be much more

19

comprehensive and include any documentation that you feel bolsters your candidacy, to include:

- an extra copy of your resume
- a business plan
- recommendations
- awards
- past evaluations
- miscellaneous items
- a "Why Me" Page

Detailed information about putting together a resume can be found in chapter 4. Here, we'll go over some of the other items you'll need to put together.

Business plan

A business plan, or ninety-day plan, is an important tool to have with you during the interview process. We have discussed the importance of preparation, and that applies to every aspect of the interview process. Of course, you need to prepare to answer potential interview questions and present your strengths in the greatest light. However, you also need to present your understanding of the business—or at least, your understanding of the steps that must be taken to build that understanding. One of the most effective tools for displaying this understanding is a business plan.

There are many effective ways to prepare and present a business plan in an interview setting. However, let's take a moment to discuss a common, less-than-optimal method for developing this tool.

During the interview process, I am commonly presented with extremely detailed, lengthy plans for conducting business. That approach is neither practical nor realistic. Regardless of the level of research you conduct on a company, industry, or business, you will likely not have the detailed inside information necessary to develop a true business plan. The company will not provide you with information such as market share, customer preferences and habits, corporate strategies, or tactics necessary to develop a proper plan. Therefore, a great deal of time is spent on a plan that everyone views as fluff. While the initiative is notable, it is unnecessary.

There are more impactful strategies that are both prudent and realistic. If done correctly, a good ninety-day plan can show a hiring manager that you have thought through the transition process and have identified key steps to quickly build your understanding of the business. A good plan will also be a useful guide to your actions upon taking a new position.

I have found, in my years of experience, that the most useful and impactful business plan format is a simple one-page document. Below are two examples of formats that I recommend be used in the interview process. In these formats, the emphasis is placed on identifying key steps that will be taken within three strategic categories.

In the first example, the strategic categories are corporate-level actions, management-level actions, and employee-level actions. Each category lists key actions that must be taken for a new employee to be successful. For example, in the corporate-level category, you need to understand things like corporate policies and corporate strategy. In the management-level category, you need to understand your manager's leadership philosophy, team policies, goals, and the like. Finally, in the employee-level category, you need to learn the basic functions and details of your new position. A new sales representative may need to develop her routing, meet her customers, and learn products. A new teacher may need to learn the code of conduct, teaching standards, and curriculum.

The second example is also an effective format and very similar to the first. The difference is the categories within which you prioritize your activities. This format categorizes actions into thirty-day goals, sixty-day goals, and ninety-day goals.

Business Plan Example 1

I. Corporate
   A. Review and understand corporate policies and procedures.
   B. Review and understand brand strategies.
   C. Review and understand corporate values and code of conduct.
II. District Manager
   A. Review and understand district goals and objectives.
   B. Review and understand district administrative requirements.
   C. Conduct strategic and tactical review of current business plans.
      1. Interpret why they are working or why not.
      2. Develop plans to mitigate obstacles.
      3. Develop plans to maximize opportunities.
III. Sales Representative
   A. Focus on quickly building product knowledge.
   B. Develop a call-routing plan.
   C. Identify key targets, business channels, and priorities.
   D. Confirm priorities with manager and hold weekly discussions.
   E. Meet and coordinate activities with co-promote partners.

Business Plan Example 2

I. Thirty Days
   A. Understand key dates: product training, technology training, etc.
   B. Conduct initial meeting with manager to understand expectations.
   C. Develop a high level of product knowledge.
   D. Conduct an initial review of my business.
   E. Develop a call-routing plan.
   F. Review business opportunities, challenges, and channels.
   G. Meet and coordinate activities with co-promote partners.
II. Sixty Days
   A. Continue to refine product knowledge.
   B. Gain a better understanding of customer needs.
   C. Meet with advocacy groups.
   D. Develop and implement promotional program plan.
III. Ninety Days
   A. Master product knowledge.
   B. Expand business with established customers.
   C. Identify new channels of business and opportunities.

These two formats are preferred because they clearly illustrate your understanding and prioritization of the key activities that must occur to ensure your success. They also demonstrate a clear, concise thought process. The one you pick is purely a matter of style.

Recommendations

Hiring managers recognize there is an inherent bias in recommendations. No one would solicit a recommendation from someone who would provide an unfavorable letter. However, recommendations still play a role in helping develop a full picture of a candidate. Recommendations from direct supervisors (past or present), coworkers, and teammates tend to provide the most value.

I also encourage the use of unsolicited recommendations to build your story line. For example, e-mails or letters from your supervisor commending you for a great job provide an excellent example of the quality of your work. As a general practice, you should gather and maintain recommendations, solicited and unsolicited, throughout your career. Recommendations do not have a shelf life.

If a manager from a previous company felt strongly enough about your work ethic and contributions to write a strong recommendation on your behalf, hold onto it. That will become one of your story lines. For example, a string of strong recommendations spread over time and different companies will contribute to a story line about your ability to succeed in all endeavors.

Past evaluations

Past evaluations typically provide some of the best insight into a candidate's performance. They provide hiring managers with your supervisor's true assessment of your work history. You should provide your most recent evaluation, at a minimum. If you have other favorable evaluations that support strong performance, include those as well.

I recommend you review your evaluation and highlight key areas that reflect strong performance. The highlighted information will help facilitate your interview presentation. For example, you would want to focus the hiring manager's attention on a section where your supervisor recorded positive comments about your work ethic or analytical skills.

Maintaining copies of evaluations is a sound habit to develop. You should be able to obtain copies of past evaluations from your current company through your manager or human resources department. However, you will likely face some challenges in getting past evaluations from previous companies. I recommend starting with your manager from the previous organization and then contacting HR if the manager can't help.

Miscellaneous items

Your brag book is fully customizable and will be the tool you rely on for success in an interview. You will be so well-versed in your presentation by the time you start developing your brag book, you will have your own ideas on what to include. Any documentation you feel bolsters your candidacy and increases the impact of your presentation is acceptable.

The primary guideline is to keep it professional. For example, letters, business documents, certificates, commendations, awards, news articles, and internship details could all contribute to your presentation. Photographs of you posing with friends at a sporting event may detract from the professional image you are trying to convey.

Think through your presentation and build your brag book to support it. Remember, the key is practice. Rehearse your presentation using your brag book repeatedly. Rehearsing will build familiarity with your materials and build confidence to a high level.

"Why Me" page

Another critical interview skill is *closing*, or asking for the job. Regardless of the type of job for which you are interviewing, it is imperative that you reinforce your interest in the job with the hiring manager and ask to go to the next step. This is something that does not come naturally to most people. I routinely witness salespeople, who close for a living, failing to close effectively in an interview setting. However, I can make this very simple for you.

The final section I recommend you include in your brag book is your "Why Me" page. The "Why Me" page is simply a summary of the key reasons for hiring you. This should be the last piece of your interview preparation.

After you have developed and tied your success stories to the job competencies, prepared your brag book, and rehearsed your presentation, you should have a very strong sense of your best selling points. These will include examples of how you meet the primary needs of the organization and why you are the best candidate. These examples constitute the "Why Me" page. The "Why Me" page should be a one-page document with bullet points that you will bring up in your closing, which we will discuss in chapter 6.

There are no parameters for this document. You may have two or ten bullets. However, develop this document with the goal of having a three- to five-minute closing discussion. Use the sample "Why Me" page below as a guide to develop your own story.

"Why Me" Page Example

1. I have a long history of well-documented, superior performance in all endeavors.
   - I excel because I'm the most driven, committed, and hard-working.
   - History is the best indicator. "Top performers don't wake up and decide to be low performers."

2. I know the market space.
   - I have a successful history within the oncology division.
   - I know how to drive business in this market.
   - I know the competition.
   - I know the payer market.

3. I have three years of account management experience.
   - I have indirect leadership experience.
   - I learned the business of health care in managed care division.

4. I have actual leadership training and experience.
   - I've led teams of from 16 to 120 people.
   - I was responsible for training, coaching, counseling, and development.
   - I've led teams in various conditions and markets.

5. I've been preparing for three years.
   - leadership: field rides, coaching, trip reports
   - business analysis
   - project management
   - interview training

6. I'm the total package.
   - field
   - TA
   - managed markets
   - leadership
   - preparation

Using your brag book

It will be important to effectively use your brag book during the interview. Remember, this is a sales presentation! The more effectively you present, or sell, yourself, the greater the chance you will win the job. You will impress any hiring manager by effectively presenting from your brag book.

There are two ways to do this. First, there will be times during the interview when, while responding to a question, you will have information in your brag book that supports your answer. You might be answering a question on past performance. During your response, open your brag book to share a supporting document on leadership. Your brag book also provides an ideal tool to facilitate closing—that is, asking for the position at the conclusion of the interview. We will discuss this point on closing later in chapter 8.

Once your brag book is complete, integrate it into your preparation. Practice using it to support responses to the sample questions. It is not enough to simply *have* a brag book; you must effectively implement this tool into your presentation for it to pay maximum dividends.

Expressing Your Interest with Research

Conveying an understanding of the position you are pursuing is a critical component of any job interview. It is imperative that you spend adequate time researching the details of the position, as well as the related company and industry. This section provides some guidelines to help focus your efforts.

Company research

Hiring managers will not expect a doctoral-level thesis on their company or industry. However, it will be important to demonstrate that you have put considerable effort into researching the company and the industry. Your primary source for information on a prospective employer is the company website. Following is some basic information you should be familiar with for the interview process:

- *General Company Information:* All corporate websites have an "About Us" section. Familiarize yourself with basic information, such as where the headquarters are located and the corporate structure—that is, whether it's an international company, where the international headquarters are located, and how the company is structured related to business units.

- *Technical and Product Information:* What current products does the company manufacture? What are its top products? What products are in development?

- *Business Units:* Does the company have multiple divisions with different target markets? For example, does it operate an electronics division, a consumer health division, and an educational products division?

- *Competitive Landscape:* Focus on the competitive landscape for the product and business unit for which you are interviewing. Be familiar with the products and some of the differences between the products. This will allow you to develop intelligent questions for the manager, such as market share differences and key selling points.

- *News Releases:* Most corporate websites have a section with recent press releases. Read through that section to identify any major news items. Maybe the company recently underwent a large expansion, launched a new product, or settled a major lawsuit. The hiring manager will see you as sophisticated and knowledgeable if you are familiar with recent corporate events.

Industry research

You will be expected to have a basic understanding of the industry in which you hope to gain employment from a functional perspective. By *functional perspective*, I mean you should have a basic understanding of how the industry is structured, how companies operate, who the market leaders are, how business is conducted, and so on. The other important aspect in conducting industry research is to gain a basic awareness of industry trends. For example, is the industry expanding or contracting? What challenges are companies in the industry facing? What is the growth outlook? As an example, let's look at the pharmaceutical industry:

- Drug manufacturers spend billions of dollars conducting research on diseases and potential cures.

- The vast majority of molecules that absorb huge amounts of financial resources fail to yield positive results and make it to market.

- Like any other corporation operating for profit, drug manufacturers have limited resources and must capitalize on new products to maintain a viable organization.

- When new products make it to market, they have limited patent lives to recoup investments.

- The largest companies are experiencing great challenges as their products lose patents.

- Technology has led to advancements in therapies, resulting in a shift from pills to biologic therapies.

- These factors are leading to consolidation within the industry as the large companies acquire smaller biotech companies to gain technology.

- The job of a pharmaceutical sales representative is to sell his company's products. His charge is to successfully differentiate his product from the competitors' products and grow his market share.

It is almost a given that you will be asked to discuss what you know about the organization with which you are interviewing. In addition to talking points, you will want to have questions about the organization prepared for the hiring manager based on your research. By focusing on the topics listed above, you should have a strong understanding of the organization and be able to have a solid conversation.

You may or may not find yourself in a conversation about the direction of the industry or challenges and opportunities faced by companies like the one you are interviewing with. However, it is imperative that you be prepared—it can make or break you in an interview.

I recall participating in a team interview several years ago when a candidate was asked about the last thing he read related to our industry. The candidate was doing well in the interview, and I thought that question could potentially send him careening off the tracks. To my surprise, the candidate responded with a story he had read that morning and told us all a few things we did not know. For the record, he was hired.

4   Creating Resumes That Stand Out

A local resume company runs an advertisement in the newspaper every week. The ad assures customers the company knows the secret to writing resumes that will get them hired into the much-sought-after pharmaceutical industry. I am not sure about that secret formula. However, as a pharmaceutical sales manager, I have reviewed endless resumes and have developed my own secret formula.

In my experience, the resumes that get noticed are not the detailed ones written on a fancy template. The resumes that get noticed are the ones written in simple form with only pertinent information provided. In fact, I routinely pass over extremely detailed resumes quickly.

Consider this story told by a fellow manager. He ran an advertisement in the local newspaper for an open position. Within a few days, he had more than three hundred resumes, not including those from recruiters and other sources. With such volume of response, it is easy to understand why overly detailed resumes are a disadvantage for job candidates.

Hiring managers have limited time and cannot review all resumes in detail. If a resume is too detailed to scan for key information, it is likely passed over. So what makes a good resume? In my experience, a good resume has two key aspects:

1. Simplicity
2. Quantifiable content

When I'm scanning a resume, I'm looking for two types of information: every position held over the course of a career, with a few key bullets under each (simplicity), and a history of success and numbers, including rankings, awards, and achievements (quantifiable content).

As we have discussed, the job market is a competitive space with many good candidates. Hiring managers are looking for the best candidate, and their first introduction to you is a quick scan of your resume. Therefore, your ideal resume will simply spell out your past experience and include quantifiable proof of previous success.

The Components of a Good Resume

I'll include some sample resumes in this chapter, but first let's look at the information you'll include in it.

Summary of qualifications

In this area, you should highlight the top qualifications and accomplishments embedded in your resume. You do not want to repeat your resume in this section, so only include select information. You should also include any pertinent experience related to the position for which you are applying. For example, if a company is looking for someone with specific experience and you have that experience, highlight it here.

Experience

This is a section where people often go overboard. There is no need to provide detailed job descriptions and minute details of your daily activities. The exception is when your job title is such that it is not common knowledge for the industry in which you are seeking a position. For example, I have reviewed resumes for people who came from a technical background. Had they neglected to provide a line or two explaining their jobs, I would not have understood their roles.

I otherwise recommend you provide dates of employment, company, position, a brief description of your job, and bullet points with key information. The information you provide should be focused more on achievements than job description. A candidate's success in previous positions carries more weight and makes more impact than a job description. If you have a track record of success, you will have the opportunity to discuss the details of previous positions in the interview.

Make every attempt to provide quantitative results on your resume—for example, "grew market share by 33 percent in 2007," or "selected as Teacher of the Year in 2010." Numbers, awards, and achievements get a hiring manager's attention.

Not everyone will have an abundance of awards and quantitative results. For example, recent college graduates have likely not had the work experience needed to accumulate meaningful accolades. Hiring managers understand that. While you may be short on work experience, you have had four years of college. Draw on your college experiences to identify areas that differentiate you from the pack. I have included some basic achievements on the sample resume for recent college graduates later in this chapter. The purpose of those entries is to help you generate ideas related to your own experiences.

There are varying opinions on how much experience should be reflected in the resume. Some suggest job candidates have some arbitrary limit on the amount of information they provide. Based on my experience as a hiring manager, I do not think you should limit yourself. When I am making hiring decisions, I want to know the person I am hiring. I am not interested in just the last ten or fifteen years, I want to know the whole person. People are very interesting, and learning about their careers and how they have developed helps me get to know that person. It helps me understand how broad and deep the candidate's knowledge has grown over the course of a career.

When I sit down with candidates for an interview, the first question I ask is that they take me back to the beginning and walk me through their career. If I sit down with someone who has ten years of experience on his or her resume but has been in the workforce longer than that, I ask myself if that individual is hiding something. My recommendation is that you include your full work history on your resume.

Another common concern is how to represent experience for someone who has been continuously employed, but only the most recent experience is relevant to the position applied for. This represents a situation similar to the previous one. You have learned, grown, and accumulated knowledge from all of your experiences. It all may not seem relevant to the position for which you are applying, but the hiring manager needs to understand your background and the broad experience you bring. That broad experience will likely be one of your story lines.

Education

School and degree are the minimum information you should provide in this section. If you had a strong GPA—3.0 or higher—include it. Also, if you had any outstanding achievements or held offices in student government or organizations, you should list those. Your year of graduation is optional and mostly irrelevant, unless you are a recent graduate with little job experience.

Other information

This is a great place to point out the importance of maintaining records. As your career progresses, you should begin collecting anything of value that you receive related to performance. You should keep recommendations, congratulatory e-mails, commendations, awards, sales rankings, project completion statistics, and any quantitative metrics related to performance. They will be very helpful as you interview for promotions or change organizations in coming years.

Attempt to keep your resume to one page if possible. However, if your level of experience is such that it warrants more than one page, that is understandable. Just refrain from including extraneous information, such as "References available on request."

Finally, spelling and grammar are always important. People who do not know you make judgments that impact your life based simply on your resume and cover letter. I will not tell you that one mistake will always knock you out of the running for a job, but it is possible. At a minimum, spelling and grammar mistakes make hiring managers question important things, such as your attention to detail, commitment, work ethic, and follow-through. It is imperative that you take the time to proofread your work to ensure it is as near perfect as possible.

Sample Resumes

General

John Doe
123 Main Street, Any Town, Any State 12345
(123) 456-7890
Jdoe@mymail.com

SUMMARY OF QUALIFICATIONS
- Four years of cardiology and infusion experience
- Ranked number 1 representative in country 2007, 2008 (143 reps total)
- Ranked number 3 representative in country 2006 (143 reps total)

EXPERIENCE

SEP 05–
Present

Heart, Inc.; Cardiology Sales Representative
- Ranked number 1 representative in country 2007, 2008
- Ranked number 3 representative in country 2006
- Winner of Team MVP Award 2007

MAR 03–
SEP 05

Biomed, Inc.; Infusion Sales Specialist
- Identified by District Manager as a management candidate
- Grew market share by 41% in 2004, highest growth in nation
- Completed management training curriculum

NOV 02–
MAR 03

Core, Inc.; Medical Sales Representative
- Promoted above seven senior representatives to spine team
- Responsible for 21% of company device sales in 2003
- Grew market share by 23% in 2003, 1st in nation

MAY 98–
OCT 02

United States Air Force; Medical Corps Officer
- Consistently rated a top officer on Officer Evaluation Reports
- Promoted ahead of peers to captain
- Gained experience in pharmacy and surgery operations

EDUCATION
United States Air Force Academy; Colorado Springs, CO
- Bachelor of Science in Chemical Engineering, 1998
- GPA–3.1

Recent College Grad

John Doe
123 Main Street, Any Town, Any State 12345
(123) 456-7890
Jdoe@mymail.com

SUMMARY OF QUALIFICATIONS
- Three months analyst training during Merrill Lynch internship
- One year of sales experience at Sun Tan Hut
- One year of coaching experience for The Runner's Club

EXPERIENCE

JUN 08–
AUG 08   **Merrill Lynch, Intern**

- Completed basic sales skills training
- Assisted broker with implementation of marketing campaigns
- Assisted with development of 9 new clients

AUG 07–
JUN 08   **Sun Tan Hut, Sales Rep**

- Top tanning package sales person 7 out of 10 months
- Increased tanning package sales by average of 28% per month
- Promoted to manager after three months on job

JUN 07–
AUG 07   **The Runner's Club, Cross-Country Coach**

- Lead instructor 75 middle-school cross-country camp students
- Developed and implemented curriculum to improve race times
- Taught importance of commitment, mental strength, and goal attainment

EXTRACURRICULAR ACTIVITIES

AUG 05–
JUN 09   **Vanderbilt University**

- University Soccer Team, 2005–2009
- Golden Key National Honor Society, 2008–2009
- Habitat for Humanity Volunteer, 2007–2008

EDUCATION

Vanderbilt University, Nashville, TN

- Bachelor of Business Administration in Marketing, 2009
- GPA–3.4

Veterans

John Doe
123 Main Street, Any Town, Any State 12345
(123) 456-7890
Jdoe@mymail.com

SUMMARY OF QUALIFICATIONS
- Ten years of leadership training and experience
- Led teams of 4 to 39 personnel to accomplish goals
- Developed training expertise as a Senior Instructor
- Possess a Top Secret SCI security clearance

EXPERIENCE

JUN 11–
AUG 13
United States Army, Platoon Sergeant

- Led team of 39 soldiers in intelligence operations
- Selected above 6 other Staff Sergeants for Platoon Sergeant position
- Consistently rated top platoon sergeant in the company

AUG 08–
JUN 11
United States Army, Senior Instructor

- Trained soldiers in intelligence processing techniques
- Selected as Instructor of the Year in 2010
- Received instruction in advanced training techniques

JUN 03–
AUG 08
United States Army, Senior Intelligence Analyst and Team Leader

- Led teams of 4 to 8 soldiers in combat environment
- Honor Graduate from Primary Leadership Development Course
- Responsible for training and developing subordinates in combat and career

EDUCATION AND SPECIALIZED TRAINING
- Defense Language Institute
- Intelligence Analyst Course
- Tactical Intelligence Operations Course
- Primary Leadership Development Course
- Basic Army Instructor's Course
- Advanced Army Instructor's Course
- Basic Noncommissioned Officer's Course

5   Developing Letters That Make an Impact

There are two types of letters you will need to master as a part of your interview preparation: cover letters and thank-you letters. One represents your first step in selling yourself for the job, and the other provides a finishing touch to all your efforts. Many job candidates fail to maximize these opportunities or ignore them altogether. Writing letters that make an impression is an easy way to put yourself at the head of the pack.

Developing Cover Letters

As discussed in the previous chapter, resumes should provide key information in a bulleted format. The cover letters that go with them provide the opportunity to *briefly* discuss those key accomplishments. There should be a tight correlation between the two documents. The purpose of the resume and cover letter is to get you in for an interview. You want to provide enough information to gain the hiring manager's interest so you can sell your qualifications in an interview.

The cover letter should never exceed one page, but the length and content will vary based on things like your experience, number of positions held, style, and personality. I will provide some basic guidelines to get you started, but I am not implying this is the only way to write cover letters. You will want to build on my guidance to develop your content in a way that reflects your own personality and conveys your desired message.

The construction of the cover letter is pretty simple. You will generally have an opening paragraph, a detailed paragraph, and a closing paragraph. You may find it helpful, as you prepare to write your letter, to think of it as a conversation. Ask yourself how you would introduce yourself to a potential employer if you were face to face. Would you go into a litany of your qualifications? You would likely open the conversation with a brief discussion about your background, transition into details about your experience and achievements, and then close with your thoughts on why you would like to fill the position. That is exactly how I recommend approaching the cover letter.

Review the job competencies for the position and identify a few key ones to focus on in your letter. Think about how your background and experience correlate with those competencies, and develop your talking points around them. The talking points will help ensure your letter maintains adequate focus on what is important to the hiring manager.

Opening paragraph

I recommend opening your cover letter with a statement about your excitement or interest in the position and why it appeals to you. Build out your opening paragraph from there with information about your current employment situation, highlighting areas or qualifications you feel demonstrate your possession of the job competencies. Keep in mind, if you do not get the hiring manager's attention up front, he may not continue to the heart of your letter.

For example, if you are interviewing for a position as a Java Developer and Programming Team Lead, you would want to highlight in the first paragraph any experience you have that relates to the job competencies. Your opening paragraph may start out similar to this:

> I am very excited about the opportunity to discuss your open position for a Java Developer and Programming Team Lead because it correlates so tightly with my background and career interests. I am an expert in Java development and spent three years as the Java training lead for new employees. I am also an expert in three other code languages. In addition to Java development, I have been the lead on numerous large-scale projects and managed the full programming department for three years.

This opening paragraph conveys your excitement about the position, but it also provides some enticing highlights of your experience that will draw the hiring manager into your letter to learn more about the details.

Detailed paragraph

The heart of your letter will be the detailed paragraph that provides specific information on some of the key qualifications in your background. Keep in mind, this is a one-page letter, so you cannot provide full details on your entire background. Your goal is to provide relevant details on the aspects of your background that qualify you for the position you are targeting. Keeping with the Java Developer and Programming Team Lead position, your second paragraph may sound similar to this:

> I have been a programmer for ten years and have certifications in SQL, PERL, Pascal, and Java. Because of my level of proficiency with Java, I was selected above fifteen other programmers for the role of Java training lead. My responsibilities included helping new employees become certified in Java, including JSP, JSF, SEAM, and Struts 1.x. As the Java trainer, I was assigned to lead multiple large-scale projects, including computer and network hardware and infrastructure, operating systems, databases, and enterprise-wide business applications. Based on my history of performance, I was selected as the manager of the programming department. In that role, I developed a full spectrum of management and leadership skills, including budgeting, oversight, teamwork, goal attainment, and employee reviews.

This paragraph accomplishes multiple goals. First, it highlights the strength of this hypothetical candidate's background, offering a good example of framing your experience to display how qualified you are. Based on this candidate's proficiency and expertise, her level of responsibility was routinely increased. Second, this paragraph highlights the key aspects of this candidate's background and ties her experience to the job competencies for the position.

Closing paragraph

Your final paragraph should simply summarize your key qualifications and interest in an opportunity to go into further detail:

In conclusion, my background and experience are extremely well-matched to the job competencies you are seeking. I am not only a Java developer, but my level of expertise led me to a training position in Java development. In addition, my extensive experience in management and project leadership will allow me to make an immediate impact on your team. I look forward to the opportunity to further discuss my qualifications with you in person. I hope to hear from you soon.

As discussed in chapter 3, you should include a copy of your cover letter and resume in the abbreviated brag book you send. You can resend the original cover letter if you desire, and that is perfectly acceptable. However, you have the opportunity to send a fresh message based on information learned from the screening process.

Sample cover letters

The sample cover letters on the following pages provide examples to help you get started. Sample Cover Letter 1 illustrates a standard cover letter as we have discussed in the preceding example. Sample Cover Letter 2 provides a good example of a letter that was developed to convey the writer's personality. I offer these two letters to illustrate the different approaches. Neither is better than the other. There is no expectation of quotes or flash in your letters. Your goal is to write a letter that reflects the message and the image you wish to convey.

One more point regarding these sample cover letters: they were written to be sent with an abbreviated brag book, as indicated by the reference to "enclosed materials" in Sample Cover Letter 2. If you have reached the point in the interview process where you are sending an abbreviated brag book, it usually means you have submitted your initial cover letter and resume, have been phone-screened, and have been scheduled for a face-to-face interview.

Sample Cover Letter 1

March 3, 2013

John Doe
123 His Street
Some City, Some State 12345

John,

I am very excited about the opportunity to discuss your open position for a Java Developer and Programming Team Lead because it correlates so tightly with my background and career interests. I am an expert in Java development and spent three years as the Java training lead for new employees. I am also an expert in three other code languages. In addition to Java development, I have been the lead on numerous large-scale projects and managed the full programming department for three years.

I have been a programmer for ten years and have certifications in SQL, PERL, Pascal, and Java. Because of my level of proficiency with Java, I was selected above fifteen other programmers for the role of Java training lead. My responsibilities included helping new employees become certified in Java, including JSP, JSF, SEAM, and Struts 1.x. As the Java trainer, I was assigned to lead multiple large-scale projects, including computer and network hardware and infrastructure, operating systems, databases, and enterprise-wide business applications. Based on my history of performance, I was selected as the manager of the programming department. In that role, I developed a full spectrum of management and leadership skills, including budgeting, oversight, teamwork, goal attainment, and employee reviews.

In conclusion, my background and experience are extremely well-matched to the job competencies you are seeking. I am not only a Java developer, but my level of expertise led me to a training position in Java development. In addition, my extensive experience in management and project leadership will allow me to make an immediate impact on your team. I look forward to the opportunity to further discuss my qualifications with you in person. I hope to hear from you soon.

Sincerely,

Sample Cover Letter 2

March 3, 2013

John Doe
123 His Street
Some City, Some State 12345

John,

An anonymous person once said, "The first principle of success is desire—knowing what you want. Desire is the planting of the seed." My desire, and my intent, is to continue building on a long history of success by becoming a top performer on your team.

I have enclosed some information to help you develop a picture of who I am and how I can contribute to your team. My military evaluations speak to my leadership abilities and my capacity to quickly master and apply knowledge in a fast-paced environment. I have also included a few of my past performance appraisals from Upward Corporation. They convey my strong business acumen and strategic approach to accomplishing goals. Also enclosed are a few unrelated recommendations from various points in time and people who have known me in different capacities. They will provide you with a broader picture of who I am.

What you will find in all of these documents is that I have a long history of rising to the top and producing superior results. From numerous ratings as a top military officer to top rankings in our industry, you will see that I possess the desire to excel, the ability to learn quickly, and the motivation, drive, and confidence that will see me to the top in any endeavor. As one of my managers wrote, "John judges himself by internal standards and does not simply keep pace with others. He holds high expectations for himself and dedicates the time and effort necessary to achieve them."

In conclusion, I have provided you with my business plan. This plan was developed based on my analysis of this opportunity and will allow for a methodical, focused approach to assessing and driving business quickly upon my assuming this position.

Abraham Lincoln once said, "Things may come to those who wait, but only the things left by those who hustle." I will continue to hustle and make things happen, hopefully for your team. Thank you for the opportunity to meet with you, I look forward to our interview.

Sincerely,

Developing Thank-You Letters

Thank-you letters are a very important component of the interview process. They speak volumes about attention to detail, follow-through, commitment, and how much the candidate cares about what he or she is doing. Most candidates write thank-you letters, so hiring managers are not surprised when they receive one from a candidate. However, I speak from experience when I say there is a degree of disappointment when an otherwise good candidate fails to make a simple, expected gesture. I encourage you to always send a thank-you letter to each person with whom you interview.

I made the statement above that hiring managers are not surprised when they receive thank-you letters because they expect them. However, there are ways to impress a hiring manager with a thank-you letter. Most candidates provide generic letters of thanks following interviews. Most are neutral; they neither improve nor hurt a respective candidate's standing in the process. With a little extra effort, you can craft thank-you letters that lead hiring managers to spend a little more time thinking about you.

You will typically spend a minimum of one hour with each person with whom you interview. Throughout a given interview, you will identify specific qualities that are important to that person when making hiring decisions. In fact, one of the questions I encourage all candidates to ask during their interviews is, "What are you looking for in a candidate?" By asking that question, you will know exactly what each person on the interview team is seeking. Make notes either during the conversation or immediately after so you have the information available when you sit down to write your thank-you letters.

Following your interviews, each person you talked to should receive a personalized thank-you letter. Each letter should highlight the qualities that person feels are important in a candidate, along with your thoughts on how you have demonstrated those qualities. For example, review the sample thank-you letter below. During this candidate's interview, the interviewer discussed the importance of leadership, business acumen, and preparation. The candidate made notes during the interview and then crafted this thank-you letter focusing on the things most important to the interviewer, along with how he met those qualifications.

Sure, thank-you letters are expected. However, this approach accomplishes many things. First, it shows interviewers you value their thoughts enough to remember them. Second, it shows interviewers that you understand what is important to them. Third, it enables you to reinforce the fact that you have the qualifications they are seeking.

Always remember to ask each person with whom you interview for a business card. Business cards provide key contact information you may need for follow-up. There are numerous options for sending thank-you letters, but the simplest and most efficient methods are e-mail or a handwritten letter.

E-mail is perfectly acceptable in today's workplace. However, the letters that have left the biggest impression on me have been handwritten and delivered immediately. Savvy candidates will handwrite a thank-you letter immediately following the interview and ask the hotel concierge or restaurant waitstaff to deliver it. I think that is a nice touch.

The bottom line with thank-you letters is, you should always send one. Regardless of the means of delivery or content, send one. I encourage you to go the extra mile and make it a quality letter. It will only help you achieve your goal.

Here's an example of what you can do to make a thank-you letter work for you.

July 29, 2013

Jill Jones
123 Her Street
Some City, Some State 12345

Jill,

Thank you for taking the time to meet with me today. I am very excited about the opportunity to work with and learn from you. Following are my thoughts on three of the key elements that came out in our discussion:

1. **Leadership:** As you have seen, I offer a significant amount of leadership experience, both direct and indirect. My ability to build teams and motivate them around a vision has been recognized in the many successful projects I have managed.
2. **Preparation:** One of the highlights of my career has been the opportunity to learn and develop under John Doe. Over the past three years, he has helped refine my skills in preparation for a specialty position. My development has focused on account-development skills, management, and leadership skills. I am fully prepared and confident that, upon assuming this new position, I will build a winning team and exceed your expectations.
3. **Business Acumen:** My previous managers consistently praised my strategic approach to business and ability to get things done. I know this space and how to drive business in this market. As we discussed briefly during the interview, I have a strong plan in place. My plan will immediately impact the territory, while setting us up for long-term success.

Again, thank you for meeting with me yesterday. I look forward to hearing from you within the next week.
Regards,

6   Positioning Yourself for the Interview of Your Life

At this point, you should feel very confident in the knowledge you have acquired. You are now familiar with the interview process, the general timeline, and the behind-the-scenes considerations that take place within the hiring team. You have invaluable insight into how managers are trained to identify and hire talented people. You understand the optimal technique for developing responses and answering interview questions. And you have been introduced to the key tools that will not only enhance your interview presentation but position you as a standout among your competitors.

In this chapter, we will focus on some of the supporting elements that are critical to ensuring that you get a face-to-face interview. We will consider a few key activities prior to your interview. We will also consider different types of interviews, including the phone interview and interviewing off your resume. These various interviews cover mostly the same content, but we will discuss some of the differences in the delivery of the content for each type.

Executing Key Pre-Interview Activities

At this point in the process, you have created answers for the sample questions; developed your brag book, including a business plan and "Why Me" page; and conducted research on the company and industry. Your primary focus should now be on rehearsing your answers and stories for the sample questions based on the BBI model.

As you rehearse, you will find that you are able to begin categorizing your answers. You will likely have multiple answers and stories for any given question. I recommend you begin categorizing your stories and answers to form a "cheat sheet." For example, consider the category "dealing with conflict." You might have numerous examples and stories that illustrate your ability to deal with conflict. Under that category, prioritize your top three answers and examples. This process can be as simple as writing the category in the margin of a sheet of notebook paper and then numbering your prioritized examples next to it.

This approach will allow you to focus and refine your preparation. You can maintain your edge by rehearsing your answers and stories as they relate to specific categories. This exercise will also facilitate last-minute preparation immediately prior to the interview by allowing you to quickly review your answers as they relate to specific categories. You might not have time to review answers to a hundred different sample questions, but you can quickly review your top answers for multiple categories.

Following are some key categories to get you started, but do not feel limited to this list:

- leadership
- success/achievements
- managing conflict
- strategic thinking
- creative thinking
- problem solving
- teamwork
- strengths
- weaknesses
- projects
- character traits

Another pre-interview activity I highly recommend is mailing copies of your abbreviated brag book to the interview team. Some candidates will arrive at the interview with a brag book in hand. That will immediately set them apart from those who do not. However, almost no one goes the extra mile of mailing a copy prior to the interview. Not only will that set you apart as having creativity and initiative, but it will allow the interview team time to review your qualifications and get to know you prior to the interview.

Either your recruiter or the human resources department for the company with which you are interviewing should be able to provide you with mailing addresses for the interview team. I suggest sending a brag book to each individual on the team, to arrive two to three days prior to your interviews. This will allow ample time to review the information, yet be close enough to the interviews to remain fresh in their minds.

Preparing to Excel in the Phone Interview

The key to the telephone screening is preparation. I recommend that you sit in a quiet room with no distractions to conduct the interview. As in a face-to-face interview, most managers will attempt to put you at ease with things like small talk and personal history. Don't be afraid to let your personality shine through; building rapport with the manager is very important. Just remember to be professional. Treat the phone screen as if you were in a business setting—keep the jokes to a minimum, and avoid things like political topics or complaints about your previous or current company.

One of the benefits of a phone screen over a face-to-face interview is the opportunity to have a "cheat sheet." This is another area where it is advantageous to have your interview stories categorized. If you are asked a specific question and the answer does not come to you immediately, you cannot quickly review a hundred sample questions to find one. However, if a question on leadership is asked and you do not have an immediate answer, you can quickly scan your cheat sheet of categories to find answers for leadership questions. I recommend you lay out your cheat sheet on your desk with your answers (examples, stories), as well as notes on pertinent company information, critical points you want to make about your qualifications ("Why Me"), and your questions for the interviewer.

There are obviously inherent challenges with phone interviews, including the impossibility of assessing or interpreting visual signals, communications, or candidates' discomfort, and the inability to share documentation. The phone interview is designed to rule out candidates who are obviously lacking in the desired skill set. The key to succeeding with phone interviews is to display enthusiasm, confidence, and the ability to verbalize your successes and why the company should move you forward in the process.

Speak confidently, loudly, and clearly. Ensure that the interviewer knows you are excited about both the company and the position. Answer questions thoroughly using the STAR format. Even if non-BBI questions are asked by the hiring manager, I recommend you answer using the BBI style where appropriate. For example, an interviewer may ask a hypothetical question like, "How would you deal with an irate customer who felt our product was of poor quality?" I suggest you respond to the question, but follow up with an example where you have dealt with an angry customer or some other form of conflict. Your detailed example will be much more impactful than a simple hypothetical response. For the sake of example, let us consider a few alternative responses to the above question.

You could provide a hypothetical response to the hypothetical question:

> I understand the importance of customer service. That is why we have a job—without our customers, we have no business. My philosophy has always been that the customer is always right. If a customer has a problem, we need to find a solution. The first thing I would do in this situation is listen to the customer to understand the problem. Once I understood the problem, I would consider all possible solutions that could be offered at my level and determine whether I could solve it. If not, I would immediately escalate the problem to my supervisor and work with her to solve the problem for the customer.

This response answers the question, but it tells the hiring manager nothing about you, aside from the fact that you are smart enough to make up a story about something that has not yet occurred. This response fails to demonstrate to the hiring manager how you have dealt with such challenges in the past. It does not allow you to demonstrate the skills he is trying to assess. Consider this alternate response:

> I understand the importance of customer service. That is why we have a job—without our customers, we have no business. My philosophy has always been that the customer is always right. If a customer has a problem, we need to find a solution. The first thing I would do in this situation is listen to the customer to understand the problem. Once I understood the problem, I would consider all possible solutions that could be offered at my level and determine

whether I could solve it. If not, I would immediately escalate the problem to my supervisor and work with her to solve the problem for the customer.

Let me share an example with you of an actual encounter I had with an irate customer. I was the floor manager for the widgets department at BigMart. When customers purchased widgets, our computer system went through a series of quality control checks that usually took three to five minutes. One afternoon, I was called to the checkout counter and was met by an irate customer. She had been waiting for her widget for twenty minutes, was late for an appointment, and was enraged [*situation/task*].

The first thing I did was apologize for the inconvenience and empathize with her. Next, I conducted an immediate systems check in front of her and was able to identify and explain the problem to her. Because of unusually high volume, the system had gone off-line. I was able to get it back online, but I explained to her that we would have to work through the backlog of customers. Every five minutes, I would personally go to the customer area, report the progress to her, and update her on how many people were still in front of her in the system [*action*].

It turned out the greatest source of her frustration was the unknown. Once I was able to figure out the problem and provide constant updates on progress, her frustration subsided. When her number came up and she came to check out, she was apologetic for her behavior. I told her I understood and apologized for the inconvenience. As an additional good-will gesture, I gave her a 5 percent discount on her widget. Not only was she happy, she became a regular customer based on the way we handled her situation [*result*].

As you can see, the second response not only answers the original question but also allows you share a specific example of a time you demonstrated the behaviors the hiring manager is trying to assess.

Finally, at the conclusion of the phone screen, use your "Why Me" page to summarize the reasons you are the best candidate for the position. Close by requesting a face-to-face interview. It is common for hiring managers to resist committing to a face-to-face interview during a phone screen because they need to speak with all candidates before making that decision. I recommend you still ask for the interview, and if the hiring manager is noncommittal, ask when and from whom you should expect to hear the next steps. It is also acceptable to ask for permission to follow up if you have not heard from anyone within the given time frame.

Learning the Keys to Interviewing from Your Resume

Some hiring managers conduct their entire interview off of a candidate's resume. They will walk through a candidate's resume and discuss it step by step. For example, they may start with college and question you about every position or move you made in order. Other managers review a candidate's resume before the interview, build their question list, and do not use the resume at all. I use a combination approach. I begin the interview with a detailed review of the resume and then follow with a more specific line of questioning.

However, in an interview using the BBI model, the goals and tactics of the interview remain the same regardless of the approach. The interviewer is focused on identifying examples from the past where you have demonstrated the desired skill set he seeks. Your charge also remains the same. Be sure to provide detailed answers in the STAR format and implement everything you have learned from this book.

The resume approach to interviewing can actually be very advantageous for the candidate if handled properly. This approach allows candidates to systematically walk hiring managers through their resume from beginning to end. The hiring manager will interject various questions along the way, but the candidate has some control.

Unfortunately, candidates are often caught off guard with this approach and fail to make an effective case for their candidacy. When using this method, an interviewer might simply ask the candidate to "walk me through your resume." Candidates frequently fail to seize this opportunity to sell themselves to the hiring manager. When candidates hear "walk me through your resume," they often point out the positions they have held in brief and look to move on. Again, remember, you are selling your qualifications.

There is a common acronym in the sales profession called "ABC." It is an acronym for "Always Be Closing!" As a candidate, you have to take every opportunity to toot your own horn—that is why you are there. This is a golden opportunity to differentiate yourself from the competition and close the sale.

Usually, an interviewer asking a candidate to "walk me through your resume" will instruct you to start with the earliest position (college or post-college) and end with the most current experience. If no suggestion is made, I recommend you follow this approach; it facilitates a good story and flow.

As discussed in previous sections, you want to paint the picture that every decision you have made has been deliberate. You review your options, weigh the benefits, implement decisively, and succeed. Begin with college: Which did you attend and why? What successes did you have? Where and why did you stand out? What lessons did you learn? From there, each job change and decision should be discussed in a similar manner. Your goal is to tell a story about who you are and how you became the person you are. Be sure to highlight all of your successes throughout this process.

We have discussed the importance of reviewing the core competencies of the job for which you are interviewing and tying your skills to them. If an interviewer asks to review your resume—and most will—it provides the perfect opportunity to capitalize on that preparation. Take advantage of this less-structured portion of the interview to demonstrate how your background and experiences correlate with the competencies for which the company is searching.

You can expect the hiring manager to raise questions as you progress through your resume. Some will simply be clarifying questions or questions of interest over some topic you have discussed. Others will be planned questions similar to those for which you have prepared. Remember to answer questions in the STAR format where appropriate.

I recommend you rehearse for two scenarios: a five-minute resume overview and an extended overview. The five-minute overview should briefly touch on the key points discussed above, including each position on your resume, lessons learned, and any key pieces of information you wish to convey. The extended overview will allow for a discussion of the full details of each position on your resume.

The hiring manager will usually provide details on how in-depth your overview should be. For example, he might say, "Can you take five minutes and walk me through your resume?" However, if no guidance is given, you should ask a clarifying question to determine the level of depth the interviewer would like to have.

Upon reaching the current time on your resume, take the opportunity to discuss why you are interviewing with the current company. Again, take the interviewer through your deliberate thought process. Make sure the interviewer knows you are excited about the opportunity and why you would be a great fit.

For example, if my goal was to be a pharmaceutical sales representative, I was interviewing with a hiring manager from a pharmaceutical company, and I had just finished reviewing my resume up to the current point in time, I might complete my comments with something similar to this:

> I am now at a very exciting point in my life. My mother worked in a doctor's office when I was a child, and I grew up in the health-care community. Many of our family friends were doctors and pharmaceutical representatives, so I was exposed to the industry at an early age.
>
> There were many things that drew my interest to this industry: the involvement in the health-care field, helping patients, and the challenging work. I am one of the few people who went into college knowing what I wanted to do for my career—be a pharmaceutical sales representative. I have spent years working to get to this point.
>
> Because of relationships stemming from my mother's position, I was able to spend my summers working with both physicians and pharmaceutical representatives. That allowed me to gain an in-depth understanding of the industry. I had the opportunity to get guidance from numerous managers in the pharmaceutical industry to prepare me for a position as a sales representative. That guidance led me to major in marketing to increase my understanding of business. Knowing how competitive the industry is motivated me to be my best. I currently hold a 3.87 grade point average.

After all of my preparation, I was amazed to see this opening with a great company like yours. You have great products to treat coronary artery disease, and your product pipeline to treat diabetes is amazing. I'm ecstatic to have the opportunity to sit down with you to discuss how I can contribute to your team.

In most cases, the hiring manager will proceed with a more direct line of questioning. If there are no further questions, expect the manager to turn the interview over to you for questions. Once the interview has been turned over to you, proceed with your questions about the company and the position; conduct a review of your qualifications via your brag book; highlight why you are the ideal candidate with your "Why Me" page; and close or ask to move to the next step in the interview process.

Sample questions to the hiring manager

The list below is intended to provide examples of the type of questions that are suitable to ask hiring managers at the conclusion of the interview. These are all appropriate questions, and you may scan through them to select any that apply to your personal situation or are of interest to you.

Hiring managers will not have time to answer all your questions in an interview. I recommend you create a list of the questions you would like to have answered, and then prioritize them. That will allow you to get the most important questions answered before running out of time.

One important note: refrain from asking any questions related to benefits and salary in the first interview. I personally reserve those discussions until we are clearly moving into the job offer phase of the process. It will usually become clear when you enter into the job offer phase. This is the point at which HR becomes involved. They will contact you to start gathering things like personal information and current or targeted salary range. As a general rule, if you are not sure you are in the job offer phase, you should refrain from discussing those topics unless the hiring manager raises them. Ask questions like these instead:

1. What is the structure of the remainder of the interview process?
2. What is the targeted timeline for the process?

3. How is training structured?
4. Why is the position open (former employee resigned, terminated, promoted)?
5. What are your expectations of new hires?
6. What are you looking for in a new hire (skills, attributes, etc.)?
7. How would you describe the corporate culture?
8. What would you change about the corporate culture?
9. What are the possibilities for advancement and career development?
10. What do you consider to be the key competitive strengths/advantages of your company versus your competition?
11. What do you consider to be the key weaknesses/disadvantages of your company versus your competition?
12. Could you tell me about your management style?
13. What skills/characteristics have you observed in your top performers?
14. Can you tell me about a typical day/week in this position/company?
15. What do you like about the company and working here?
16. What would you change or improve about the company and working here?
17. What are the career paths in this position/division/company?
18. What are the most pressing actions that need to be taken once this position is filled?
19. What is your view of the competitive situation?
20. What are the market share and growth trends for the territory for which I'm interviewing?
21. What are the territory rank and most recent quota attainments?
22. Who are the early adopters in the territory?
23. Who are the high-volume nonadopters?
24. What is the specific call panel (who will I call on)?
25. What are the growth opportunities for the territory?
26. Is the company involved in any co-promotions for its products?
27. What has/has not been done to drive business in this territory (special projects, programs, etc.)?
28. What are the national market share and growth trends for your product?

Executing the Close

Many people fret about the dreaded interview close. However, if done correctly, it's a very simple and natural process. To ensure you have time for this critical component, it is vital that you point out at the beginning of the interview that you have a few things you would like to share. Ask the hiring manager if he or she will reserve a few minutes for you at the end of the interview. It is standard practice to allow time for a candidate's questions at the end, but sometimes interviews run long and candidates' questions are cut short. Making this request up front will help ensure that the hiring manager allots adequate time for your close.

At the end of the interview, when the hiring manager turns it over to you for questions, be sure to ask at least a few intelligent ones. If you sense you're short on time, simply let the interviewer know you have more questions, but out of respect for his time, you would like to summarize some important points. At that point, I recommend you take a few minutes to flip through your brag book and reinforce some of the highlights. Then go to your "Why Me" page and take the hiring manager through your list of why you are the best candidate.

Conclude by asking the interviewer if he has seen anything that concerns him about your candidacy. If he has concerns, I recommend you ask what they are and address them appropriately. If he has no concerns, ask if he will send you to the next step in the process. It is that simple!

Do not be intimidated by the close. As with all other components of your interview presentation, it is important that you rehearse for this final moment. The more you practice, the easier it will be and the more naturally it will come off.

7 Developing Answers with Sample Interview Questions

As you begin preparing answers for the questions in this chapter, you will find your list of story lines, actions, and examples growing. Keep in mind that your goal is to create a catalog, both mental and written, of examples of past performances that you can mentally scan for answers during your interview.

The list below is not exhaustive. There is no way to predict what questions a hiring manager will ask in an interview. However, these are actual interview questions. They cover a broad range of categories, scenarios, and behaviors. By developing your catalog of answers and practicing with the questions below, you will create a list of individual answers.

Each individual answer may pertain to an unlimited number of unique questions. So when a hiring manager asks a question you have not heard before, instead of panicking, you will simply go through your mental file and select the most appropriate, preconceived answer.

Develop answers for all of the following questions. If you come up with more than one answer for a question, add all of them to your list. Once your list is complete, continue to review it in relation to the questions below. The more familiar you are with your answers, or catalog, the more relaxed and confident you will be during the interview.

Remember, when answering questions, apply the STAR format where appropriate. Also, remember to quantify your answers and be as specific as possible. For example, your proud response to a question might be the fact that you had the highest sales growth in your district in your previous position. It would be much more effective to share the fact that for the eight salespeople in your district, average monthly sales growth for the year was 10 percent, with a range of 7 percent to 16 percent. You had the highest average in the district, 16 percent, with a personal range from 12 percent to 22 percent. The second response not only displays your superior performance but also shows that you understand your business.

Recent college graduates should approach the development of their responses in the same manner. Though you might not have as much work experience to draw on, you have four years of college experience. Develop your answers around class projects, group projects, summer jobs, internships, athletics, and any other experience you might have gained over the last four years.

Your goal is the same: to show that you possess qualities that will lead to success. The venue where your qualities were displayed is not as important as having displayed them. I recall one candidate who focused on her success while working a summer job at a tanning salon. She presented a table showing how many tanning packages she sold compared to the other employees. She broke it down into growth percentages month-over-month and also showed by how many percentage points her sales exceeded each of the other employees. Her success not only displayed the desirable qualities companies seek, but her presentation of the information displayed strong communication skills and strong business acumen. She successfully earned a position in her targeted industry before graduating from college.

This chapter is broken into two parts:

1. Behavior-based interview questions
2. Additional interview questions

Although the STAR format should be used whenever possible, it is not appropriate for all interview questions. For example, "What is your GPA?" or "What are your career goals?" can't be answered using the STAR format. I have included a list of common non-BBI questions in this section to complete your preparation.

Because my background is in sales, many of these sample answers are related to sales scenarios. Obviously, a recent college graduate or a person from a nonsales background will have responses related to their specific backgrounds. What is important is developing answers that reflect your individual achievements and successes in life.

Behavior-Based Interview Questions

1. Can you tell me a little about yourself?

This is not really a BBI question, but I'm including it here because most hiring managers begin their interviews with something similar. It's not meant to elicit information on your favorite food or vacation destination. Instead, it allows candidates to open with a simple question and break the ice, so to speak. It also allows the hiring manager to get an initial look into your past decisions. Your answer should be concise. A rule of thumb is to limit your answer to this question to three to five minutes.

A good starting point for people who have been in the workforce for a few years is usually college. Your answer should display clarity of purpose, decisiveness, and success. You might discuss the thought process by which you chose your college, what steps you took to increase your odds of admission, and what you accomplished and learned while there. Then, transition into post-college activities, such as jobs held and charitable or community organizations in which you participated. Again, discuss the rationale for your decisions and what you accomplished and learned.

Conclude your answer with how and why you developed a desire to enter the targeted industry and company, and what steps you have taken to achieve your goal. For recent college graduates, a brief personal history may include where you grew up, high school activities and leadership roles, your college experience, jobs held, and areas where you excelled. For example, perhaps you worked at a tanning salon part-time while attending college. You could highlight such achievements as selling the most tanning packages, customer service and employee recognition awards, and promotion to shift supervisor. Your goal is to review all of your achievements and build a detailed story around them to display how focused, detail-oriented, competitive, and superior you are. Whichever case applies, remember to quantify achievements where possible.

2. Can you give me an example of your strategic thought process or strategic approaches you have taken to achieve your goals?

This question gives you the opportunity to display your ability to strategize and determine the best course of action in a given situation. Develop your answer to show that you can look at the big picture and drill down to specific actions that will produce your desired results.

Sample Answer

I was once promoted into a position selling a product that was used for both Crohn's disease and celiac disease. In my new territory, sales had decreased consistently over the previous four quarters [*situation/task*].

I conducted a detailed analysis of the territory and discovered the previous sales representative had focused on the market for Crohn's disease. I also discovered that, based on volume, there was far greater opportunity for growth in the market for celiac disease. I implemented a new strategy to maintain my business for Crohn's disease while shifting my primary focus to developing the celiac-disease market. I developed a call cycle that allowed me to see all of my customers two times per month. I also held three educational programs per month and had an educational lunch with each customer once per month [*action*].

I discovered that my customers were unfamiliar with my product's use for celiac disease. Once educated on the potential benefits, they were willing to try it. The results proved to be very strong, and my customers were very satisfied. As a result, I grew sales in my territory over the next year by an average of 15 percent per month and won an award for sales excellence [*result*].

3. Can you give me an example of your creative thinking process or creative approaches you have taken to achieve your goals?

This question is similar to the previous one, but the interviewer is trying to find out whether you have the ability to determine different, creative approaches to accomplish your goals in spite of obstacles.

Sample Answer

In my territory, I had responsibility for an office of five buyers. Each of the buyers was a high-volume purchaser of my competitor's product line and represented a great opportunity for my business. However, their office policy prevented sales representatives from interacting with them directly [*situation/task*].

I spent several months building a relationship with the office secretary and gaining valuable information about the office. At one point, I learned of an industry expert who was very much respected by the buyers. The expert was a huge advocate of my product line. I asked the secretary to send a note to the senior buyer asking if I could bring this expert to their office for lunch. The buyer was ecstatic and said he would love the opportunity to meet with the expert [*action*].

Over the next several months, I brought in four different industry experts for lunch at the office. As a result, I developed very strong relationships with the five buyers and their staff. I was able to switch their business from my competitor's product line to mine, and my sales grew by an average of 15 percent per month for the next nine months [*result*].

4. Can you tell me about a time you were given negative feedback and how you dealt with the feedback?

This is one of many questions designed to explore your personality type. Specifically, this question helps determine whether you are coachable and willing to learn or if you will be a challenge to manage.

Sample Answer

My mother worked as an office manager in a physician's office while I was growing up. I spent a great deal of time in the office over the years and had considerable time to observe and interact with pharmaceutical representatives. Their jobs seemed challenging, yet very interesting. By the time I started college, I knew that I wanted to pursue a career as a pharmaceutical representative.

At the end of my junior year of college, I began trying

to network with hiring managers in the pharmaceutical industry. The first manager I spoke with gave me very discouraging feedback. His response to my interest in the industry was that my lack of sales experience would prevent me from getting hired. He recommended that I take a job in another industry for a few years to get some experience [*situation/task*].

I was determined to earn a job in the pharmaceutical industry right out of college. I spent time strategizing ways to build my resume and enhance my experience. The first thing I did was take a summer job selling tanning packages at a local salon. Next, I contacted a pharmaceutical representative and invited him to lunch to share his expertise. We put together an action plan for the summer that included a schedule for me to shadow him at work [*action*].

The shadow experience was invaluable. I learned basic sales skills, tips on professional interactions, presentation skills, and the realities of the position. I also gained great sales experience at the salon. Over a four-month period, I grew my tanning-package sales by an average of 18 percent per month. My sales numbers were improving every month. During my first month on the job, I grew sales by 5 percent, but by the fourth month, my sales growth was more than 20 percent. I won the Summer Sales Champ award for having the highest sales volume over the May to August period.

That first manager's negative feedback proved to be a great impetus for increasing my preparedness for a position in the pharmaceutical industry [*result*].

5. Can you tell me about a time you had to sell your boss on something? What approach did you take? What was the result?

A critical skill is the ability to "sell up." Many times in your career, you will have very good, creative ideas to grow your business. However, your manager may not see the value in your proposed idea. Your success will hinge on your ability to persuade your manager that your idea will lead to success.

Sample Answer

A national industry group hosts an annual convention every January. Typically, one sponsor has the coveted opportunity to provide an expert speaker who is usually an advocate of that sponsor's product. Other sponsors are left with opportunities to provide less impactful speakers for small-group discussions. My company worked with a celebrity speaker, and the convention chairman requested to have that celebrity speak at last year's convention. My boss initially declined because of the costs involved [*situation/task*].

I explained to my boss that, based on the costs involved, I was able to negotiate with the convention chairman. If we brought in the celebrity speaker, she would be the keynote speaker. In addition, the convention chairman was also willing to let us provide an additional expert speaker. Historically, the convention attendance averaged ten thousand people. This convention provided us with the opportunity to provide the two key speakers, create a very favorable company message for a large group of people, and impact national sales [*action*].

Ultimately, my manager agreed that the ability to impact so many people with two key speakers was worth the cost involved, and we implemented the plan. Over the three-month period following the convention, our national sales spiked by an average of 12 percent per month [*result*].

6. Can you tell me about a time you bent the rules for the good of the customer? What was your rationale? What was the outcome?

This question assesses your critical reasoning and decision-making skills. Companies are not looking for rebels. However, customer service is a critical element for companies.

Sample Answer

I had been negotiating a contract with a customer for three months. We had finally reached an agreement and were meeting for lunch to sign the document. The contract department was behind schedule and mailed the documents overnight to my hotel. I received the documents just in time to leave for the meeting. As I crossed the street to the office to meet with my customer, I noticed the contract department had added verbiage to the contract that we had not discussed or agreed upon [*situation/task*].

I took my customer through the contract and pointed out the discrepancy. I was not authorized to change contracts, but I allowed the customer to write in that the contract was void unless the added verbiage was removed. Following the meeting, I immediately contacted my manager to explain the situation and the actions I had taken [*action*].

My manager agreed with my decision and contacted the contract department to rectify the situation. My customer was thankful and appreciated my integrity. He signed the contract, and I was able to work out the issue favorably with my company. Ultimately, we not only accomplished our goal, but gained the trust and respect of an important customer [*result*].

7. Can you tell me about a management decision that you disagreed with and how you handled the situation?

This question explores your conflict resolution skills. Invariably, you will have disagreements with your manager, coworkers or subordinates. Hiring managers are looking for people who handle disagreements in a mature manner. Remember to frame all responses professionally, with no complaining or derogatory comments.

Sample Answer

My manager once directed me to begin developing new detailed reports for my customers based on a format she had received during a recent training course [*situation/task*].

I respectfully explained that the new report seemed redundant. I provided supporting information for my argument in the form of other reports that contained the same information. I felt the exercise duplicated our efforts and decreased efficiency [*action*].

After hearing my concerns, she provided her rationale for the request. The end result was that I respected the fact that, as a manager, she had business needs that required her to take certain actions without justification. I was allowed to voice my concerns, but ultimately began creating the new reports as requested [*result*].

8. Can you tell me what you consider to be your greatest contribution to your company/position? Why? Can you give some details of how this was accomplished?

This is an opportunity to highlight your key successes with your current or previous employer, or in school if that's all the experience you have. Prepare answers for several key contributions, as variations of this question may come up over the course of an interview and you will want to have fresh examples. Examples of key contributions might include a unique project you developed that led to positive changes at your company. If you were in a sales position with a previous company, a great contribution might be above-average sales performance. For recent college graduates, your greatest contribution might include athletic or academic successes. Again, remember to structure your answers using the STAR format.

Sample Answer

I consider my greatest contribution to be my success in the field. When I took over my current territory, it was ranked last in the nation. During the interview process, I told my future manager that I was a performer and would turn around the territory [*situation/task*].

Upon assuming responsibility for the territory, I spent a great deal of time analyzing the business. I identified where I was losing business and where my greatest opportunities were. I initiated an educational programming initiative to jump-start my business [*action*].

My efforts led to my ranking as one of the top three sales representatives in the country for three consecutive years. I was hired to grow my business, and I have excelled at what my company asked of me. I feel that is my greatest contribution [*result*].

9. Can you tell me about a time you failed to accomplish a goal? Why did you fail? What did you learn from the failure?

We all have experienced failure at some point in our lives. This is not designed to be a "gotcha" question. The key to developing an answer for this question is not to hang on the failure, but rather to expound on the lessons learned from the failure and how you have grown from the experience.

Sample Answer

My first job after college was a sales position. I am very competitive and ambitious by nature, and my goal was to be the top sales representative in my company. At the end of my first quarter with the company, the sales results and rankings were distributed. My stomach dropped when I found myself ranked number seventy-six out of seventy-seven representatives. My initial thought was that my career was over before it had even started [*situation/task*].

At that point, I sat down and analyzed my business. I determined where I had made an impact the previous quarter, who and what were the key drivers of my business, and where my call routing could be optimized. I analyzed my competitors' data and refined my messaging, and I believed I was capable of turning around my territory [*action*].

When the sales results and rankings came out for the next quarter, I had risen from number seventy-six to number two in the entire nation. The lesson I learned is that commitment and knowledge are two of the keys to success. Commitment to success and making the effort to master all aspects of the business yielded great dividends [*result*].

10. Can you tell me about a problem you solved, what process you employed, and what the outcome was?

The goal of this question is to assess your ability to identify a problem, develop possible courses of action, war-game those possible actions, and then choose and implement a successful solution.

Sample Answer

During college, I was in the Army ROTC program. The senior cadets (fourth year) ran the program under the guidance of the cadre. We conducted numerous overnight training exercises as a department, which included cadets from freshmen to seniors. As the cadet-in-charge, I began receiving concerns from the lowerclassmen. They charged that during our training exercises, the lowerclassmen were expected to adhere to army standards, while some groups of upperclassmen were not expected to adhere to standards [*situation/task*].

I gathered the senior cadets to discuss the issue and collect information. I found out that the seniors felt as though they should not be expected to adhere to standards because "we are in charge." I was told this was a "rite of passage" and things had "always been done this way." I led a discussion on leading by example and pointed out that it is more important than ever to adhere to standards when you are in charge. Your entire subordinate unit will fail to uphold standards if they feel standards are not important to their leader. I explained that failing to lead by example because that is "how things have always been done" was a poor excuse [*action*].

The group discussion proved to be a great lesson in leadership. In the end, we all agreed that as future military officers, it was important to uphold and enforce standards. For the rest of my senior year, all upperclassmen adhered to the same standards as the lowerclassmen [*result*].

11. Can you tell me about a mistake you made? How did you handle it? What did you learn from it?

Hiring managers know you have and will make mistakes. This is another opportunity to see into your thought process. Did you admit to a mistake and take actions to correct it? Did you learn from your mistake and improve your performance as a result? Can you articulate and illustrate what you learned and how you improved?

Sample Answer

My company once created a special pricing strategy for a select group of large organizations. As sales reps, we were tasked with testing the waters with these organizations to ascertain whether they would have an interest in pursuing a contract under this new strategy [*situation/task*].

I discussed tactics with my fellow sales reps, and we all agreed that we would have to provide some limited details of the strategy to the targeted organizations in order for them to determine their level of interest. I approached one of the targeted organizations and, as we had agreed, shared details of the strategy [*action*].

The organization leaked details of the strategy to another organization with which we already had a contract. That organization was offended that we were offering more advantageous pricing to the larger organization and threatened to cancel our contract. The result was a huge upheaval within my company.

I had a strong relationship with the organization that

leaked the strategy. They had nothing to benefit from the leak and intended no ill will. It was ultimately a series of mistakes made on all sides of the table, and we were able to salvage the deal. The lesson for me was to confirm tactics prior to execution to ensure that there will be no unexpected consequence [*result*].

12. Can you tell me about a good sales call you've made in the past? Why was it good, how did it develop, and what was the outcome?

This will apply if you have a sales background. If you do not have a sales background, you may be asked to discuss a past success.

Sample Answer

I was a fairly new sales rep, having been in the field for less than six months. John Jones was one of the top targets in my territory. He was difficult to see and even more difficult to engage in discussion. Over a period of three months, I had multiple conversations with him about my product but felt I was getting nowhere. I had spent time reviewing a new study related to my product class and felt it was the information I needed for a breakthrough [*situation/task*].

My manager was with me on my next call with Mr. Jones. Upon opening the call, I discussed the evidence in the new study that reported that my product was effective in three applications, where the competitive product was effective in only one application. We had a lengthy discussion on the various applications and effectiveness of each product. Following our discussion, I asked why he would use any other product [*action*].

John Jones then looked at my manager and me, paused for a moment, and said, "You got me." I was surprised and asked for clarification. He went on to tell me he agreed with the new data I had presented, and he would begin using my product in the future. Over the next six months, he converted 97 percent of his business to my product [*result*].

13. Can you tell me about a bad sales call you made in the past? Why was it bad, how did it develop, and what was the outcome?

This question may be rephrased to focus on a mistake or poor job performance for those in a nonsales position. It allows the interviewer to assess many aspects of your personality and performance. For example, it explores how you deal with customers, whether you are self-aware and realize when you make mistakes, how you react when mistakes are made, and whether you can self-coach to identify improvement areas.

Sample Answer

Once, while working with my district trainer, I made a call on Dr. Smith, one of my top three targets. I was very aggressive in discussing the features and benefits that I felt made my product the best. The customer seemed to listen intently. However, at the conclusion of my presentation, she abruptly told me she was out of time and had to go. In the follow-up discussion with my district trainer, he asked, "Did you notice how angry she was?" [*situation/task*].

After that call, I took my trainer to the airport and then sat in my car analyzing the call with Dr. Smith. As I thought through it, I realized that my aggressive approach was far too direct for that customer's personality style. I thought back on successful calls with her in the past and how I dealt with her in those calls. I determined that she was an amiable/analytical personality type and required a much softer selling approach. I left the airport and returned to the customer's office to apologize for the aggressive nature of the earlier call [*action*].

Dr. Smith was impressed that I made the effort to return to her office to apologize. She said that she had never seen me act that way in the past and attributed it to the pressure of my trainer's presence. As a result of our interactions that day, we gained a new mutual respect, which led to increased access, a strengthened relationship, and market-share growth for my product [*result*].

14. Can you tell me about the worst decision you ever made? How did you handle it, and what was the outcome?

No one is perfect. We all make mistakes. The important aspect of this question is how you handled the situation, what you learned from your mistake, and how you implemented the lesson going forward.

Sample Answer

Early in my career, I had a large account with multiple targets split between two locations. The staff and management in one location were friendly and easy to access. However, the staff and management at the other location were quite the opposite. As a result, I spent considerably more time and resources on the more accessible office, which resulted in sales growth. At one point, the office administrator requested a meeting with me. She demanded that I "owed" her staff at the other office several lunches based on my activities at the accessible office [*situation/task*].

Acting on principle, I explained that it was a large office, and it was very costly to provide them all with lunch. I further explained that when I had done so in the past, no one had spoken with me. I went on to question the business rationale of such an expensive endeavor when no business could be discussed [*action*].

As a result, I was prohibited from returning to the office. However, I learned an important lesson from this mistake. Principles are very important, but you have to choose your battles. It would have been more effective to access the office via lunch meetings and improve relationships to the point where business discussions could have been conducted. Ultimately, we worked through our differences, and I developed strong relationships in both offices [*result*].

15. Can you tell me about a conflict you have had in a professional setting and how you handled it? What was the outcome?

This is another question designed to assess your conflict resolution and interpersonal skills. Hopefully you do not have stories of great conflict. However, everyone faces minor conflicts in a work setting at some point. With this question, hiring managers are trying to elicit examples to gain insight into your personality and how well you interact with people. They want to know if you will be disruptive for the business, the customers, or the team.

Sample Answer

I once had conflicting views with my manager over how to handle a contract issue with a top customer. The customer had just signed a supplier contract with a competitor of mine. Our primary product was similar, but my product had multiple delivery options that allowed the product to be used in multiple ways. Only about half of the end-users were able to use my competitor's product because there was just one delivery option and alternatives were needed. I suggested offering a supplemental contract to the customer that would allow them to offer my product to customers who needed an alternative delivery device. My manager immediately refused the idea on the basis that we do not sign contracts for secondary positions [*situation/task*].

I conducted some research and gathered data from my customer. I presented a very strong case in which I showed two things. First, half of the end-users were unable to use the competitive product and had no options. My recommended contract would allow us to immediately gain 50 percent of a multi-million-dollar market. Second, it allowed us to create a partnership with the customer and get a step closer to becoming their primary supplier [*action*].

Ultimately, my manager agreed that the opportunity was very strong, and we closed the contract. Within thirty days, we gained 50 percent of the business. The contract gave us an opportunity to begin working closely with the customer to demonstrate the value we provided, and six months later we won the contract to be the exclusive supplier in our product class [*result*].

16. Can you tell me about a time you had to implement a new approach or plan because your initial approach was not working?

Oftentimes we develop strategies based on available information and implement what we believe to be the best decisions based on our analysis of a given situation. However, once implemented, we find those strategies aren't optimal and need to be adjusted. This question looks at your ability to make and implement sound decisions, as well as your insight and flexibility in adjusting and refining decisions.

Sample Answer

As a manager, I once had an employee whose skill set was below average. During customer interactions, I noticed that she never had answers to their concerns and seemed to be generally uninformed [*situation/task*].

My initial approach to correcting the problem was to conduct individual meetings with her to discuss her business in more depth and to focus on how to meet customer needs. After about three months, I noticed the employee had become increasingly nervous around me, and it was manifesting in a combative attitude. I realized that the increased focus in our individual meetings was making her feel singled out and incompetent. This was a good employee, and my intent was to help make her better. I immediately changed my approach to spend more time with her in front of customers to demonstrate by example the qualities I was trying to develop in her [*action*].

In the month following my new approach, she began to relax and better understand my expectations. She spent time improving her knowledge in areas that she identified as being important to customers. Slowly, she began taking the lead in our customer interactions. Within three months, she had developed to the point where I had full confidence in her customer interactions, and we were able to return to a normal work routine [*result*].

17. Can you tell me about a time you had to take on a leadership role to accomplish a goal?

Leadership is a critical trait at all levels of an organization. It is common that people need to display leadership with peers, with coworkers over whom they have no authority, and in many varied situations to accomplish goals. This question helps interviewers explore a candidate's leadership abilities.

Sample Answer

At my previous company, we co-promoted our primary product with another company. When I assumed responsibility for the territory, it was ranked last in the nation. I soon discovered that a great deal of hostility existed between the two companies' sales forces. We had a team of four sales representatives, and each wanted to do things his or her way. It was a very counterproductive situation, and the sales results showed it [*situation/task*].

After observing the behavior for a few weeks, I invited the other three representatives to dinner to discuss a new strategy. We spent time discussing general business and territory issues. I then led a discussion on the importance of collaboration and teamwork. We all agreed that our current behavior would not produce the results we wanted. We established new business rules and committed to increased communication and business planning, and overall improved team efforts [*action*].

Ten months later, our territory had risen from last in the nation to number three. We were also recognized at a joint national meeting for our teamwork and high functionality [*result*].

18. Can you tell me about a time your product had a disadvantage (such as higher price or side effects) but you were successful anyway?

This question speaks to your resourcefulness and ability to clearly differentiate and sell the benefits of your product.

Sample Answer

Our product was the last of five products to enter a highly competitive market, and it was the most expensive. My competitors routinely pointed out the fact that we were more expensive and would require customers to pay even more money for an already expensive product. As a result, many accounts refused to stock our product [*situation/task*].

Although my competition was talking about our higher price, they failed to point out the rationale for the premium pricing. We had conducted head-to-head studies that proved our product worked far better and lasted longer than the products available from our competitors. During my first nine months in the territory, I conducted more than fifty educational programs. I also conducted more than a hundred lunch presentations. I developed a highly focused call plan and made every possible effort to educate my accounts on the benefits of our product over the competitors' [*action*].

Over the next twelve months, my accounts accepted the premium pricing on our product because I was able to display superiority over competitive products. Within a year, our product became the market leader in my territory [*result*].

19. Can you tell me about a time when you played a role in a team success?

Teamwork and strong interpersonal skills are important in most professional environments. The purpose of this question is to determine how well you work with others. Do you contribute to the team? Do you take over the team? Hiring managers are not looking for examples of when you single-handedly saved the world. They are looking for examples of when you were a good team player and helped a team accomplish a goal.

Sample Answer

When I was working as a regional account manager, the sales manager and his sales team in my region were responsible for selling a product that was not available through the top supplier in the region. As a result, their success in the area had been very limited [*situation/task*].

We worked together as a team to develop a course of action. We developed action items for each member of the team. The sales representatives committed to sales activities, and the manager committed to tracking his team's progress and guiding their efforts. My job was to get the supplier to stock our product. We built a list of tactics that included identifying the decision maker within the supplier organization and coordinating a meeting with local buyers. I began calling the supplier's switchboard and talking with secretaries. At one point, a secretary was able to tell me the name of the general manager and provide me with his secretary's phone number. After multiple discussions with the secretary, I was able to convince her that my meeting with the manager was important for both their business and their customers' business [*action*].

She gave me an appointment, and I was able to persuade the manager of the importance of meeting with his customers to hear their concerns. Six weeks later, after multiple meetings at all levels, the manager agreed to begin stocking my product [*result*].

20. Can you tell me about a time you wish you had acted differently with someone at work?

This is another question that explores your interpersonal skills and professionalism.

Sample Answer

A new customer moved into my territory and had been conducting business there for about a year. In his effort to effectively transition his customers from his previous location in another state, he was traveling to his previous office a few days each month. At one point, the customer suddenly dropped from my database. After researching the issue, I discovered that the sales representative from his previous location had been successful in having him added back into her database [*situation/task*].

I had put a great deal of effort into building his advocacy for our product, and he had become a great advocate for us. Based on my efforts over the past year, I strongly objected to the change. When the district managers were unable to resolve the issue, I requested it be escalated to higher levels [*action*].

Ultimately, it was recognized that the customer practiced in my territory and that I had worked with him extensively. He was added back into my database, but I felt like my relationship with my coworker had been damaged. I think the escalation and damage could have been prevented if I had worked directly with my coworker from the onset [*result*].

21. Can you tell me about the most difficult (or simplest) task you have had to learn? Why was it difficult? How did you approach it? What was the outcome?
This question provides insight into two important areas. First, it enables hiring managers to assess your capacity for mastering complex information. Second, it provides insight into your problem-solving approach. How do you prepare to tackle complex issues? How focused are you? How do you manage setbacks? Think through the various educational moments in your past. For example, think of tasks you have had to learn when starting new jobs, project teams on which you have participated, or hobbies where you have developed an interest that blossomed.

Sample Answer

One of the most difficult tasks I have had to learn was when I was in the military. I served in the Intelligence Corps, and when I first arrived at my duty station, I was assigned to a highly complex piece of equipment that I had never seen before. I was told my job was to become an expert on the equipment, and the expectation was that I "get up to speed, ASAP" [*situation/task*].

I began working with a seasoned operator to learn on the job. However, to learn the system as quickly as possible, I took some additional measures. I spent my off-duty time reading various technical manuals and learning the specifications and capabilities of the system. That enabled me to better understand the lessons learned from the other operator while on duty. I also spent time working additional shifts to gain insight from other operators and gain more experience [*action*].

About two weeks after reporting to my duty station, I overheard my supervisor telling our commander what a fast learner I was and that he was impressed with how quickly I was learning the system. Within two months, I became a primary operator, and within six months, I was training others on the system [*result*].

22. Can you tell me about a situation where you had to overcome serious obstacles to achieve success?

Again, this question provides insight into your ability to break down problems and find ways to win. Provide in-depth details on the issue and the actions taken to resolve it.

Sample Answer

At one time I assumed responsibility for a new area that was dominated by one large buyer group. When I entered the office for the first time, the receptionists were rude and informed me that the group didn't see sales reps [*situation/task*].

For several months, I made visits and tried to get past the receptionists. I developed a fair relationship with one of them and ultimately was able to capitalize on it. On one visit, I asked the receptionist if she would at least give Mr. Smith, the head buyer, a note from me, and she agreed. In the note, I offered to bring in an industry expert from London to have lunch with his group in his conference room. At that point, he came out to meet me and ask if I could actually get the expert to come. Over the next six to eight months, I brought in industry experts monthly to meet with the large group [*action*].

I was able to spend time with the buyers coordinating and participating in the lunches. My relationships grew very strong and allowed me to share the benefits of my products. As a result, my market share soared in the office, and I finished number two in the nation that year [*result*].

23. Can you tell me about a time when you were expected to adhere to policies with which you disagreed?

Corporate policies are not only designed for good business practices, but also to ensure that organizations and personnel are operating within acceptable legal parameters. Managers do not want to hire people who have difficulty adhering to policies. This question also provides insight into your personal values and morals.

Sample Answer

I currently work in a highly regulated industry. Last year, my organization announced it was taking a leadership role within the industry by banning all entertainment with our customers. As we were the only company adopting these stringent rules, our sales representatives were put at a great competitive disadvantage [*situation/task*].

There was a great deal of displeasure with the decision. I requested a position on the CEO's advisory panel so that I could discuss, and possibly influence, the decision. I discussed it with my fellow sales representatives to gain a broad range of opinions. I spent time refining and rehearsing the delivery of our concerns. I also discussed them with my manager to ensure that they were valid and grounded in solid business strategy. At the advisory meeting, I represented my team's concerns respectfully [*action*].

Ultimately, the new rules were placed into effect. However, I felt satisfied that I was involved in the process and was allowed to discuss my team's concerns. I initially felt limited by the new rules. However, with a continued focus on the benefits of my product, I've grown my sales by 13 percent this year [*result*].

24. Can you tell me about the most competitive position in which you have competed?

The purpose of this question is not to hear about a competitive environment, but rather, how you operated and succeeded in a competitive market. It is not necessary to have an example in the field in which you are seeking employment. It is just a look at how you function and excel in a competitive environment.

Sample Answer

The most competitive position in which I've competed was in the BPH market. It was a small market, and there were four modalities competing for the business. We had the first product to market and had built a loyal following. However, the three new companies had strong data behind their products. Every order made a big impact, and the competition was intense [*situation/task*].

My assessment was that I had to be moving at all times. My personal efforts were critical, but they needed to be supplemented by all available resources. I developed and implemented a strong strategy. I conducted programs to educate the buyers on the benefits of my product. I conducted programs to educate the suppliers on my products. I participated in local society events, advertised in newspapers, and mailed out information. I was successful in building a buzz around my product that made an impact at events even when I could not be present [*action*].

My strategy proved very successful. Not only did I grow existing business, but I was able to win back customers who had gone to my competitors. My product became the recommended product of the state advisory panel, and my business grew an average of 22 percent over the past two years [*result*].

25. Can you tell me about a time in which you had to prioritize to accomplish many tasks in a short period of time?

This question explores your ability to function in a busy position when there are numerous demands on your time. Can you multitask, or do you need to focus on one task until it is complete?

Sample Answer

In January 2007, I was promoted from a specialty sales rep to a hospital sales rep. Both were very demanding positions. I was asked by my previous manager to maintain my efforts and business in my previous position for four to six weeks while he backfilled my position. During that time, the specialty sales force announced an expansion, and my previous manager became incredibly busy, which lengthened his hiring process. I worked both my old and new position for five months [*situation/task*].

Initially, it was stressful trying to learn a new position while performing my previous job. I maintained two separate planners to keep from confusing appointments. I also maintained separate journals for each position to ensure that I was capturing pertinent details and information. Each day I would dedicate time to focusing on my previous position. If phone calls or e-mails came in related to my previous position, I would record them and focus on them during that dedicated time [*action*].

I settled into a routine and functioned smoothly. I was successful in both learning my new job and maintaining the business in my old position. When a new specialty rep was eventually hired, I had an updated calendar of appointments and a detailed journal containing pertinent notes and business issues. That allowed for a smooth transition for the new rep and allowed me to focus on my new job [*result*].

26. Can you tell me about the last thing you had to teach yourself on the fly? How and why did you do it? What was the outcome?

This type of question is designed to assess your thought process and how you approach problems. Do you take a logical, well-conceived approach, or do you shoot from the hip? The subject is not as important as the process. The sample answer below is a notable example from a recent interview.

Sample Answer

I recently decided to update the trim and baseboards in my home. I called a few experts for estimates and was stunned to discover it would cost approximately $12,000. I'm not exactly a handyman, but after reviewing the estimates, I decided I would attempt the job myself [*situation/task*].

The first thing I did was take some measurements and price materials to ensure that the money saved on labor was worth my effort. Next, I spent a few hours in the bookstore reading home-improvement manuals to develop a base of knowledge. I then went to the home-improvement store to discuss the project with the help desk. Once I felt like I had learned enough to begin the project, I decided to get started [*action*].

I knew I would make some beginner mistakes, so I chose to start in an upstairs closet where they wouldn't be noticed. I did make a few mistakes on cutting the angles to match the boards in the corners. However, with some practice, I was proficient at the job. The project took about six weeks to complete. However, in the end, I saved money, developed a new skill, and gained a sense of satisfaction from the job I had done [*result*].

27. Can you give me an example of a time you were given a task and, on your own, went above and beyond the call of duty?

Hiring managers are looking for employees with a high level of commitment. This question helps explore a candidate's willingness to put in extra time and effort to exceed standards.

Sample Answer

In my previous company, the sales reps were charged with working closely with industry experts to ensure success with large buyer groups. When our products came up for review, we would have experts come in to present to the buyer committees. I pointed out to my sales manager that all of the experts did the same thing: they typed up a two- or three-page document, looked down, and read it to the committee. I questioned whether they made any impact. I suggested that an expert with a few key slides that could be discussed with the committee members would be much more impactful [*situation/task*].

As a sales rep, I was very familiar with our needs at the committee meetings. I spent several days developing a five-slide deck from scratch. I pulled key data points that I thought would be meaningful to the committee to create the new slides. I submitted them to my sales manager, and he submitted them for internal approval [*action*].

The new slide deck was approved, with some minor changes, and we had a new approach to the committee meetings. I worked with my sales manager and industry experts on the most effective way to present the new deck. We developed a presentation that was far superior to the previous presentation. The expert with whom I worked trained the pertinent people in our company so everyone understood the new approach. To date, we've used the new approach in seven committee meetings and have been successful every time [*result*].

28. Can you tell me about an important goal you set recently and what you have done to accomplish it?

This question simply explores how you set goals and develop plans to accomplish them—and whether you actually do accomplish your goals.

Sample Answer

I have set a short-term goal of earning a position as a pharmaceutical sales representative and a long-term goal of rising to a management-level position within the pharmaceutical industry [*situation/task*].

To improve my skill set and better position myself for both positions, I've initiated work on my MBA. I researched local schools, determined which program was the best fit for a professional with a full-time job, took the GMAT, and applied to Johns Hopkins University [*action*].

I'm currently two semesters through a four-semester program and expect to graduate in December 2010 [*result*].

29. Can you describe some obstacles you have faced in your present or most recent job? How did you handle them and what was the outcome?

The purpose of this question is not to list shortcomings with your current or former organization, but rather to explore how you deal with adversity.

Sample Answer

Our previous approach to selling to large buyers had become obsolete. Upon securing appointments with an organization, our sales reps would meet with the buyer committees individually. They would discuss contract issues, technical information, competitive information, and any other information required. However, the industry and product lines had grown. The scope of the information required became too much for individual sales reps to manage alone [*situation/task*].

I recognized the dilemma early, and upon securing an appointment with a larger buyer, I began to strategize. To ensure success, I developed a unique plan. My goal was to develop a team approach to my customer meeting. Ultimately, I presented market dynamics and then had a contract manager present our proposal and options. I brought in an industry expert to discuss product differentiation and an economist to discuss underlying cost concerns [*action*].

The customer was incredibly impressed and stated that it was the best product meeting he had ever participated in. We successfully negotiated the contract, and the approach was adopted as the new company standard [*result*].

30. Can you tell me about a time you went outside the scope of your job to help a team member?

Teamwork is very important in almost all organizations. Everything from sharing best practices to simply building a strong, supportive team is affected by each individual. Hiring managers want to see that you are willing to put your personal interests aside for the good of the team.

Sample Answer

I was once contacted by a coworker with whom I had worked very closely. He had met a vice president of a large organization in the Northeast. Our product was not stocked by that organization, and the VP wanted to implement a change. Because of internal issues, he was facing a stiff challenge and needed our help. However, he had attempted to work with our local sales rep and felt she was not supporting him. He refused to work with her going forward. My coworker had assured him that I could help solve his problems and asked me to work on the issue with him.

The organization was located outside my territory, so success there was of no personal benefit to me. In fact, I had to seek special authorization internally to be allowed to work the account. However, because a teammate had requested my assistance, I offered to do everything I could [*situation/task*].

I cleared my calendar to meet with the VP for several hours to gain an understanding of his organization, his problem, what had been done, and what I could do to help him achieve his goal. At the conclusion of the meeting, we had developed an action plan. I conducted several internal briefings, interfaced with the VP, and eventually put together a team that could help [*action*].

The team that I helped form took the reins on the initiative with the VP, and within six months our product was being stocked by his organization [*result*].

31. Can you tell me about a time you realized your manager needed coaching or feedback in a certain area? How did you handle the situation?

This question explores interpersonal skills. It provides interviewers with insight into how you interact with people in general, and more specifically, how you interact with authority.

Sample Answer

I once had a manager who wanted to schedule a team meeting on Halloween. I reminded him that several of our reps had children, and Halloween was a big event for them.

I suggested moving the meeting forward a day to allow for this family event. His response was that we all missed special events; it was part of the business, and I needed to get used to it [*situation/task*].

I explained that I had been in the industry for ten years and certainly realized that missing special events was sometimes unavoidable. I further explained my thinking that since this was not a national meeting but a team meeting being coordinated by us, we had the opportunity to avoid such a situation and should take it [*action*].

He told me the meeting was going to be scheduled for Halloween and that was final. He called back later and told me he'd thought about our discussion and agreed that we shouldn't choose to penalize ourselves if we have an option. The meeting was moved ahead one day, and everyone was home for Halloween [*result*].

32. Can you tell me about a time you lost a sale, contract, or business?

This question provides the hiring manager with an opportunity to evaluate your thought process from another perspective—how have you dealt with a loss, and what actions did you take to turn the situation around?

Sample Answer

I had a situation where I lost a contract, but with some strategic action was successful in winning it back again. I received a request for a proposal from a large account in my territory. They were reevaluating their product line and all the suppliers in my product class were attempting to seize the opportunity. After discussing the issue with a buyer from the account, I discovered that they planned to recommend to their committee that our product no longer be stocked because of weak demand [*situation/task*].

I organized a local team that consisted of the sales manager, the sales rep, and me. We met with local end-user groups to discuss the issue and explain why our product was one that should remain available. We met with the account to explain the differences in our product and why it should remain available. We also brought in an industry expert for the committee meeting to present the product differences to the committee [*action*].

When it came time to vote, the committee announced its decision to remove our product from the product list. After a brief pause, one committee member raised his hand and recommended adding our product back to the list based on some key benefits it offered. The committee agreed, and we were added back to the product line [*result*].

33. Can you tell me about a time you solved a customer problem and defused a difficult situation?

Customer service and interpersonal skills are critical to all organizations. This question explores the candidate's ability to manage conflict and solve problems.

Sample Answer

I once had difficulty gaining access to a key account. The account had several hundred employees in multiple departments, and it was very important to my business. The person in charge met with me once to let me know he saw no need to ever see me again.

After months of attempts to break through with the account, they approached me about support for a new conference they were planning. Seeing this as my opportunity to partner with this important customer, I committed to introducing them to my company's funding process. I met with the person in charge, presented a brochure that walked them through our process, answered questions, and left them with contact information for future questions.

I thought everything was set ... until I received a phone call from the account complaining because we had too many gaps in our process. The customer felt like I should not have presented this option if we didn't have a full solution. My opportunity was not only slipping away, but I was in a worse position simply for trying to help [*situation/task*].

After careful consideration, I contacted a third-party organization and explained what the account was trying to do. The third party said they would love to work with my customer and could provide a full solution. I shared all the details regarding my account's goals, answered questions, and committed to coordinating the introduction [*action*].

I was able to contact my customer and explain that I had identified an organization that could provide a solution for their problem. I put the two organizations in contact with each other, and the event was ultimately very successful. The customer was grateful that I was able to assist them in achieving their goals, and my access improved greatly [*result*].

34. Can you tell me about your experience dealing with a difficult customer? What made the customer difficult, and how did you handle it?

This is another example of a question that helps interviewers explore a candidate's personality with regard to interpersonal skills, conflict management, and customer service.

Sample Answer

I had a large account that did not carry my product, and I had targeted it as a growth account. However, the senior buyer for the organization was nearly impossible to see. He was well-insulated by his staff and would only meet with sales reps for extraordinary reasons [*situation/task*].

I spent six months trying to reach him, to no avail. I contacted staff, peers, and friends. I spent time in areas where I thought I might run into him. I perused the corporate website looking for anything that might be useful. At one point, I found a collection of minutes from past committee meetings on the website. As I read them to gain insight into this important customer, I found one sentence that stated the senior buyer wanted to see a presentation comparing the products in the class to which my product belonged.

I went straight to his secretary and explained that he had requested the presentation and I would like to provide it. I was given an appointment and began preparing for a "one shot" meeting. I presented market dynamics and the competitive landscape. I had an industry expert attend to present the differences in the products and their applications. I had an economist attend to discuss underlying costs and future savings. I had a vice president attend to reinforce my company's commitment to the business [*action*].

The account was extremely impressed with the presentation. After reviewing the information, the senior buyer stated that he planned to add my product to his line. I have since built a good relationship with him and now have open access and a growing market share [*result*].

35. Can you tell me about the last time you had your integrity tested?

Obviously, integrity is a very important issue in these litigious times. Hiring managers want to know that you are trustworthy. They also need to know you won't go outside company guidelines while conducting business, potentially involving the company in a legal issue.

Sample Answer

I once sold a product for which we provided samples. The intent of the samples was to allow the account to provide product demonstrations. I was approached by a customer who requested additional samples with the intent of selling them for a profit. He indicated that if I provided the samples, his use of my product would grow [*situation/task*].

I reiterated our corporate policy on sampling and let

him know that I would not deviate from the guidelines. I reported the discussion to my corporate headquarters to raise awareness, and we stopped providing samples to the customer in question [*action*].

The customer explained after our discussion that he fully understood our corporate policy. He committed to refraining from his suggested activities, but I explained that I was uncomfortable with the situation and would no longer provide him with samples. He understood and respected me for taking a stand [*result*].

36. Can you tell me about a decision about which you deliberated for a long time before deciding? Why was it difficult? How did you make a decision?

Again, you want to show that there is some structure to your decision-making process.

Sample Answer

It was a very difficult decision for me to leave the air force. I was a successful officer, had built a solid start to my military career, and enjoyed the sense of purpose and teamwork. However, I had a strong drive to test myself in the corporate world [*situation/task*].

I spent months reading books about civilian career fields to determine which path I would like to pursue if I chose to leave the military. I contacted former officers who had made the transition to discuss their thoughts and experiences. After identifying pharmaceutical sales as a desirable career, I spent time on the job with a rep to gain experience. I discussed my thoughts with my wife and made the decision to pursue a civilian career in the pharmaceutical industry [*action*].

I made a smooth transition and have had a very successful career. I've risen through the ranks and held multiple management-level positions. I am certain that I made a sound decision to leave the military [*result*].

37. Can you tell me about a time you involved others in helping with a difficult decision?

Teamwork is a critical skill that hiring managers seek in candidates. This question explores how well you work with others, as well as your ability to use all available resources to accomplish a goal.

Sample Answer

As a top sales rep in my organization, I was once given an offer for a sales training position within my company. It seemed like an exciting opportunity, but I was ambivalent about accepting it. I enjoyed my current position as a sales rep and wasn't sure how much I would enjoy an office position. It would require relocation to an expensive area of the country. I had children in school and lived near family. There were a lot of factors, and the decision was difficult [*situation/task*].

The first thing I did was talk with current and previous trainers to get their insight on the position and working in the office. I spoke with my manager to get his input on career advancement and the importance of the training position. I spoke with peers to get their thoughts on the transition. After gathering all the information, I spoke with my wife and shared the feedback I had gathered [*action*].

Ultimately, I decided that I was happy in my current role. Though the offer was exciting, I did not want to relocate my family and had no desire to work in an office setting. I respectfully declined the offer [*result*].

38. Can you tell me about a time when you requested assistance from coworkers on a project or assignment?

This question provides another opportunity to explore a candidate's propensity for teamwork and ability to bring all resources together to achieve goals.

Sample Answer

I had been calling on my top account for almost a year and had no success getting in to see anyone. I had a contact at another account who was a former employee of this top account. He attempted to call in some favors, but I still was unable to access the account. I spoke with secretaries on a regular basis, but they were never successful in securing appointments for me. I attended industry meetings and attempted to get time with someone from the account during the breaks. Nothing was working [*situation/task*].

I asked fellow sales reps in my district to join me in a teleconference to discuss the difficult account. We discussed the various approaches I had taken and then shared ideas on other tactics I could employ. At one point, a fellow sales rep made a very simple suggestion. She suggested that I just show up at the account and request to see someone. I had tried everything else and felt that the worst that could happen was to be told no. I decided to start with the vice president's secretary. I had spent the most time talking on the phone with her. Within a few weeks, I walked into the account. After getting through security, I asked to speak with the secretary. I heard her laugh over the phone when security told her I was downstairs, and she agreed to come down [*action*].

Ten minutes later, she walked up and introduced herself. She told me she had bumped into the vice president on her way down and asked the VP to come and meet me. I spent fifteen minutes with the vice president and her secretary. From that point, I never had another problem securing an appointment. Within six months, my product was added to their product line, and my sales grew by 17 percent per month for the next fifteen months [*result*].

39. Can you tell me about the best idea you've sold, your approach, and the result?

All positions, regardless of the industry, require employees to sell their ideas. Creativity and persuasion are important traits in any capacity, and this question allows interviewers to explore those skills.

Sample Answer

At a previous company, we worked with a celebrity spokeswoman who was using our product. She would participate in meetings in large metropolitan areas where approximately two hundred people would attend. My territory was in a rural area, and I never had the opportunity to have one of the spokeswoman meetings [*situation/task*].

I discovered an annual event in my area that three hundred to four hundred people typically attended. I approached my manager with the idea of creating my own spokeswoman meeting in conjunction with the event. Initially she refused, based on the location in a rural area. I pointed out that we would have a higher attendance than what they get in the larger metropolitan areas. She authorized me to pursue the meeting but didn't think it would happen. I spent three months making phone calls, conducting teleconferences, and researching resources like hair and makeup artists. Finally everyone agreed to conduct the meeting [*action*].

The attendance for the event exceeded five hundred people and set a new record that year. We had a great program that led to a 47 percent increase in my sales that year, and I was able to build some great new relationships [*result*].

40. Can you tell me about a time you changed your position on an issue as a result of feedback from others?

This question explores your ability to work as part of a team and allows the interviewer to seek out personality traits like flexibility, understanding, empathy, and the ability to acknowledge when there is a better way.

Sample Answer

My team once had a contest that involved having our accounts mail letters to their customers about our product. I was one of the first sales reps to have an account agree to conduct the mailing. When I notified my manager of my success, he requested a copy of the letter that was sent [*situation/task*].

I felt that asking my account for a copy was unprofessional and showed a lack of trust. My stance was that I would forgo the contest credit rather than question my customer [*action*].

However, the following week we had a team discussion on the issue. One of my fellow sales reps voiced the opinion that we should view all information that was sent out regarding our company. She had seen letters in the past that had incorrect information and wanted to prevent it from happening again. After listening to the discussion, I realized there was, at a minimum, a need for quality control in the mailings. Based on feedback from that fellow rep, I began asking to review the mailings before they were sent [*result*].

41. Can you tell me about a time you have had to establish yourself and build relationships as a member of a new team?

This question explores teamwork and interpersonal skills. Hiring managers want to know how you will integrate yourself into your team and with new customers. This question gives them insight into how you approach those situations.

Sample Answer

I've always found that hard work, modesty, and integrity are keys to building trust and respect. I found myself in this situation when I joined my current team. My entire division was formed only one year prior to my joining the company. Shortly after formation, the new sales force launched our company's flagship product in an extremely competitive market. The eight other reps on my team had been together since the launch of the product and had developed a strong bond. I was not given a very warm reception; they treated me like an intruder [*situation/task*].

Although I was new to this team, I had been in the industry for several years and knew how to drive business. My first priority was to make an impact on sales. I immediately implemented an educational programming strategy that would ultimately earn several awards. My manager began highlighting my successes and asking me to discuss my strategies during team meetings. When I discussed my ideas, I remained very modest and deferred to their experience. I used phrases like "you guys have probably done similar programs" or "I'm sure you've thought of this." As my sales continued to increase, I began receiving calls from teammates asking about what I was doing. I was very open and willing to share ideas to help anyone I could [*action*].

I began building individual relationships. I recall at a national meeting overhearing one of my teammates say to another, "He's one of us," meaning they then saw me as a member of the team [*result*].

42. Can you give me an example of when you have implemented feedback?

Hiring managers prefer to hire candidates who are open to learning. This question allows interviewers to assess a candidate's ability to learn and implement new ideas and ways of doing things.

Sample Answer

As a sales rep, part of my job is negotiating contracts with accounts. However, I don't have free reign in negotiations. My company has internal controls in place to ensure that the contract makes good business sense. Before presenting a contract to an account, I must first conduct a contract presentation to our internal contract department. If my presentation makes an acceptable business case for the contract, it will be approved. If I fail to make an acceptable business case for the contract, it will not be approved.

When I conducted my first contract presentation, I spent weeks working on the presentation. I felt I was well-prepared and had built a sound case for my proposal. The presentation seemed to go well and was ultimately approved. However, after the presentation, my manager asked if I had just put it together the night before. He understood it was my first proposal, but he told me very directly that it did not meet the standard [*situation/task*].

After receiving my manager's feedback, I became a student of the contract presentation. I called my fellow reps and asked them to send me their latest presentations. I studied each one, took from them what I liked, and built my own presentation [*action*].

I received great praise from my manager on my next presentation. After I had conducted several more, he appointed me as the trainer for contract presentations. Senior reps were required to consult with me on their presentations before presenting them internally [*result*].

43. Can you describe the greatest challenge you've faced in a job and how you dealt with it?

The way you overcome adversity and obstacles reflects key traits like tenacity, perseverance, and a drive to accomplish goals. Those are traits that hiring managers find very desirable in a candidate, and this question helps them explore that aspect of your background.

Sample Answer

One of the greatest challenges I've faced in a job was making the transition from a sales rep to a specialty-products rep. As a specialty-products rep, I was expected to operate at a management level. Suddenly, my administrative requirements increased exponentially. My performance expectations also went up sharply. I found myself interfacing with vice presidents and directors; my presentations were expected to be perfect. I had product sales reps and sales managers coming to me for advice and guidance on buyer committee issues, and I was expected to have answers [*situation/task*].

Initially, the change was intimidating. I immediately took steps to learn my business inside out. I read books on specialized selling and studied existing contracts to understand current positions. I also took a course focused on conducting presentations for corporate officers. I then set up meetings with each of the teams I supported to conduct an initial presentation on the business we shared [*action*].

My confidence grew with each success. Each strong presentation made to a vice president or successful meeting with the sales team increased my knowledge and experience, and I started operating at a higher level. I became a very successful special-products rep and won our company's top sales award during my second year in the position [*result*].

44. Can you tell me about a time you had to develop a solution, new idea, or suggestion for a project or job?

This question allows interviewers to examine critical-thinking skills and creativity, gaining insight into a candidate's ability to analyze a situation, develop an effective course of action, and implement the solution.

Sample Answer

I was once working on a project with a large account in New York. They had implemented a new policy that placed all of the products for my product class on their high-cost product list. My goal was to gain a favorable position for my product, but the new policy presented an obstacle [*situation/task*].

I met with the senior buyer to determine the limits of the new policy. I then discussed it with my fellow reps to get their input on possible solutions. After careful analysis, I presented an option to the account. Through my analysis, I was able to show the institution that they would achieve greater cost savings by making my product the preferred product on their high-cost list. It was actually the lowest-cost product on the list. It also had the highest dependability score. If it was the preferred product, they would save costs on things like returns and fielding customer complaints [*action*].

They were intrigued by my analysis but wanted to conduct their own. Upon completion of analysis by their contract department, they agreed with me and accepted my proposal [*result*].

45. Can you describe how you organize and track multiple tasks? How do you stay focused?

In today's fast-paced environment, people are expected to manage numerous priorities or projects at any given time. To successfully accomplish that, they must have strong organizational and time-management skills. This question allows interviewers to assess those skills in a candidate, as well as determine the candidate's ability to prioritize.

Sample Answer

In my current capacity, I support eight managers, thirty-two sales representatives, and six technical experts across four divisions. My job is to develop new business and negotiate contracts with new customers. I have to maintain technical expertise for the product line from each division and also work with the respective sales representative to coordinate customer events, such as promotional programs. Once new contracts are signed, I'm responsible for developing and executing activities to increase sales for the newly contracted product. In addition to field-level activities, I conduct weekly activities related to analysis of current business and forecasting of future business [*situation/task*].

My organization skills are strong and invaluable. I maintain detailed computer records as well as a binder with hard copies of pertinent information for backup. I also maintain to-do lists and tactics sheets for each product/ division. My tactics sheets list key activities that must take place along with the person responsible for that tactic. That allows me to keep everyone on task [*action*].

As you can see from my yearly evaluations, I do all of these things very successfully. Section three from my evaluation for last year highlights my strengths in organization skills and shows that I finished the year ranked the number-one account manager in the nation [*result*].

46. Can you tell me about a time you functioned as part of a team and what contribution you made?

This question provides another opportunity to assess a candidate's teamwork and collaboration skills. It also gives the interviewer a look at the role a candidate plays on teams. Some people are leaders and some are technical experts. Consider the role you play and be able to explain the value you add in a team setting.

Sample Answer

As a specialty-products rep, my entire job was an exercise in teamwork. My primary role was working with the senior buyer to negotiate contracts. To that end, I developed a team selling model that became the standard for the sales force across the nation. I had been working to gain an appointment with the senior buyer in a large account for more than a year. At one point, the buyer got a new secretary who was much friendlier than the previous one. I met her on her first day and began working with her immediately. After about six weeks, I was notified that I would be given a thirty-minute appointment with the buyer [*situation/task*].

Typically, I would conduct the product presentation and the proposal presentation myself. However, as I weighed the magnitude of this opportunity, I wanted to create every chance for success. I worked with my manager to put together the strongest team possible. We had an industry expert attend to present the data behind the product. We also had an economist attend to present the total cost comparison. I then had a representative from a relevant local society present the need to make our product available to patients. Finally, I presented our proposal [*action*].

The presentation was so impactful, we were put on formulary within two months. Our display of teamwork was so effective that it became the national standard [*result*].

47. Can you tell me about a crisis situation you had in a job? How did you respond and recover?

Urgent crisis situations will arise in all organizations and positions. The outcome of those situations is typically in direct correlation to how a given employee responds, especially where customers are involved. This question allows interviewers to assess a candidate's ability to remain calm, react favorably, and make sound decisions in a crisis.

Sample Answer

As an account manager, I was responsible for negotiating contracts for my company's services. I had defined parameters, but I also had the freedom to operate within those parameters for the good of my organization. Contract terms were typically decided based on a variety of factors, such as account size, volume, and whether an account agreed to use my company's services exclusively.

I had reached an agreement with an account and was waiting for my contracting department to provide paperwork to finalize the deal. When it was ready, my assistant mailed the contract to the account to be signed. The following day, I received an irate phone call from the account. My assistant had mistakenly included paperwork with the contract that detailed our deal with another customer. The new account was upset because their deal was not as good and threatened to cancel our agreement [*situation/task*].

I immediately went to the account after receiving the phone call. My approach was to reason with them from a business perspective. I explained that the primary difference in the two contracts was that the other account was willing to enter into an exclusive agreement with us for our services. I was unable to offer equal terms on a contract that was less favorable for my organization [*action*].

After settling down, the contract manager understood that different business circumstances dictated different contract terms. However, the mistake led the account to reconsider our original deal. I was able to show them they would have no decline in service by going with our company exclusively, and the move would result in great savings for them. In the end, they received the same contract terms as the other account and we gained another exclusive customer [*result*].

48. Describe a time when you were faced with a stressful situation. How did you react and what was the outcome?

This question is similar to the one related to managing crisis situations and allows interviewers to assess a candidate's ability to function under stress.

Sample Answer

I had a very successful year in 2009. I had exceeded all production goals, as well as all individual performance goals my manager had put in place for me. As a result, I was given an award by our CEO for exemplary performance. We had a company-wide meeting scheduled for February 2010 to kick off the New Year. A week prior to the meeting, I was asked to participate in a telephone conference with the vice president of our division. The vice president told me that he had selected me to accompany him onstage during our February meeting. His intent was for me to spend a few minutes addressing the division to share the keys to my success. The challenge was that I had never spoken in front of anyone other than the eight people on my team. As the day grew closer, I became more nervous [*situation/task*].

My first thought was that preparation would help alleviate any anxiety. I prepared a brief overview of the actions I believed contributed to my success. After I had organized my thoughts, I prepared a cheat sheet with bulleted comments and began rehearsing. As a contingency plan, I developed a few simple closing comments to get me out of the situation if things went badly [*action*].

The fateful date came, and as I walked into the auditorium and saw hundreds of people, my stomach tightened up. Shortly after opening the meeting, our vice president made some remarks about success and then invited me to join him onstage. I did as I had rehearsed, and my talk was going well. Suddenly, I made eye contact with a friend and completely lost my train of thought. Initially, I got very nervous and thought things were about to go bad. However, I knew I had prepared a contingency plan to get me out of the situation if needed. Knowing that I was well-prepared and had a backup plan enabled me to relax. I took a deep breath, finished my comments, shook the vice president's hand, and exited the stage. I had successfully given my first talk in front of several hundred people [*result*].

49. Describe a situation where you faced significant barriers to success and how you overcame those barriers. Did you succeed?

Hiring managers are looking for employees who possess the ability to accomplish goals, regardless of the level of challenge faced. This question allows interviewers to assess a candidate's ability to find acceptable ways to achieve goals despite barriers.

Sample Answer

After college, I went into the military for four years. After completing my obligation, I decided to enter into the civilian workforce. However, I was uncertain as to what career options were available. After a great deal of research, I decided that I wanted to enter pharmaceutical sales. The work seemed challenging, interesting, and potentially lucrative. The challenges I faced stemmed from the fact that I had never been in sales before. In fact, I didn't even have basic business experience. The only post-college experience I had was in the military, and I didn't feel that experience prepared me for a career in sales [*situation/task*].

I had the self-confidence to believe that I could accomplish anything I attempted. During the two-month period between leaving the military and beginning my sales career, I became a student of the sales profession. I read multiple books, spent significant time researching sales techniques on the Internet, and attended a sales conference. Upon entering the pharmaceutical-sales profession, I was put through sales school, but I still had little practical experience. During my first six months in the field, I had daily calls with my trainer to help reconcile my book knowledge and training with actual experience [*action*].

At the conclusion of my first six months in the field, I

climbed to number two in the nation in the sales rankings. As I have discovered, the sales profession involves constant training and development. I never feel as though I know everything, but I have been able to overcome significant challenges to become a top sales representative in my industry [*result*].

50. Can you tell me about a time you fell short and did not achieve your goal or desired outcome?

As important as your successes are when you're selling yourself in an interview, hiring managers know that occasional failures are inevitable. This question allows them to see how candidates acknowledge and deal with disappointment.

Sample Answer

My primary goal in college was to benefit fully from the broad range of opportunities and experiences that were available. I was an officer in my fraternity, participated in many of the campus clubs and intramural sports, and belonged to the Golden Key National Honor Society. One of my interim goals during my junior year was to win a position in the Student Government Association [*situation/task*].

I mobilized my fraternity and initiated a social campaign. We attempted to leverage every connection and contact possible. I had an article published in the school paper, blanketed the campus with fliers, and spent time introducing myself and talking with fellow students. I felt my odds for success were above average [*action*].

On election day, I fell short and was not elected to the position for which I campaigned. However, it was a good experience, and I learned some great lessons. For example, I learned to effectively leverage social networks to impact a cause. Ultimately, I had a great time and made many new friends [*result*].

Additional Questions

After reading through fifty BBI questions and answers, you should have a strong sense of how to formulate answers and apply the STAR format.

I have listed additional questions below to facilitate an even higher level of preparation. Many of these questions are behavior-based, but I have also included some of the more common interview questions that are not behavior-based. As discussed previously, the BBI model is the most demanding form of interviewing. By preparing for this model, you will be well-prepared for any other model. Reviewing the full list of questions below will further enhance your preparation. Remember when formulating your answers that everything you have done has been well-planned and deliberate. Develop your answers to support the skills you want to project and ensure you include lessons learned from each experience.

More BBI questions

1. Can you tell me about a situation in which you were able to persuade someone to see things your way?
2. Can you tell me about a difficult decision you have made in the last year?
3. Tell me about a time you recognized that you needed help on a project or task.
4. Can you give me an example of a time you took the lead and showed initiative?
5. Tell me about a time you applied information you learned in one of your college courses to your work.
6. Can you tell me about a time you worked with an individual you did not get along with but had to for a work or school project?
7. Can you tell me about a time you assumed accountability for a task and results outside of your position and responsibility? What was the situation? How did you demonstrate that you took responsibility for the results? What were your objectives? What difficulties did you encounter? What did you do to resolve issues? What was the result?
8. Tell me about a time you had to take disciplinary measures with a subordinate.
9. Tell me about the most challenging project or assignment you received. How did you manage it? What steps did you take?

10. Tell me about a time you were not pleased with your work, such as a project or assignment. How did you respond?

11. Tell me about a time a fellow student or coworker was not doing his or her share of the work on a project. How did you respond? What was the outcome?

12. Tell me about a time you had to take an unpopular stance regarding something you believed in. What was the result?

13. Give me an example of a time when you set a goal and were able to achieve it.

14. Tell me about a time when you had too many things to do and you were required to prioritize your tasks. How did you determine priorities? Did you accomplish all the tasks?

15. Give me an example of a time when you had to make a quick decision. What was your thought process? How did you approach the situation?

16. Tell me about a time you had to win the trust and respect of a person or team.

17. Tell me about a time you had difficulty with a manager or instructor. How did you resolve it?

18. Tell me about a time you had to help develop the skills of another person.

19. Tell me about a problem or challenge you recently faced. How did you resolve it?

20. Tell me about a project you delegated to a subordinate to aid in his or her development.

21. Tell me about a time you had to provide negative feedback to a subordinate.

22. Tell me about a time you had to work with someone outside your team to accomplish a goal.

23. Tell me about a time you disagreed with someone on your team about a problem, solution, or business matter. How did you handle it? What was the outcome?

24. Can you tell me about a time you anticipated problems and took preemptive measures? What measures did you take to prepare for and overcome potential problems?

25. Tell me about a situation you feel you could have handled better.

26. Can you tell me about a time you had to learn something on the fly? How did you do it? What was the outcome?

Non-BBI questions

1. What are your expectations of yourself in school or work? What have you done to ensure that you meet or exceed those standards?
2. Tell me what your dream job would be if you could create it.
3. What are your greatest strengths?
4. What are your greatest weaknesses?
5. What are your career goals?
6. What do you know about our company?
7. Are you willing to relocate?
8. Tell me about the one accomplishment in your career or college that you are most proud of—what is it, and why did you choose that?
9. What drives you to succeed?
10. Are you better at working on many things or hammering out results for a few things?
11. How would your peers describe you? What would they say are your strengths and weaknesses?
12. Describe your current team. What do you like and dislike?
13. Describe your current manager. What do you like and dislike?
14. How do you earn respect from your peers and coworkers?
15. What qualities differentiate successful people from unsuccessful people?
16. Tell me about the greatest challenge you've faced.
17. Do you think that your grades are a fair representation of your academic achievement?
18. What do you know about our company?
19. Why do you want to work for our company?
20. What quality or attribute do you feel will most contribute to your career success?
21. What personal weakness has caused you the greatest challenge in school or work?
22. What is the last book, article, or magazine you've read?
23. Where do you see yourself in five years?

24. Tell me about a time you missed a deadline. Why did you miss it? What did you do?

25. What do you think it takes to be successful in this career? What have you done to prepare?

26. Tell me about your greatest accomplishment.

27. If you could, what would you do differently in your college or career experience?

28. Do you prefer to work as an individual or as a member of a team?

29. Give me an example of a time when you motivated others.

30. Tell me about a time when you delegated a task.

31. Tell me about your goals—long-term, short-term, career, and personal.

32. How have you helped a department you supported run more effectively or efficiently?

33. What do you enjoy in your free time—what are your hobbies?

34. What motivates you?

35. Why should I hire you over someone with more experience?

36. Describe the greatest challenge you have faced.

37. Tell me about your extracurricular activities. Why and how did you get involved? What have you gained from the experience?

38. Can you tell me about your awards, academic or otherwise? What did it take to win those awards? How did you achieve success?

39. What was your GPA? Class rank?

40. Can you tell me about your work experience gained during college, such as summer jobs and internships? How did you choose those jobs? What did you gain from those jobs?

41. Can you tell me what activities or educational experience you feel has helped prepare you for the workforce?

42. What are the most impactful, life-shaping events of your life so far?

43. Which college class did you enjoy the most and why?

44. How did you choose which college to attend?

45. What was your major? Why? How did you arrive at that decision?

46. How has your college experience prepared you for a position in this company/industry?

47. What type of manager do you prefer and work best with?

48. How do you prioritize and manage multiple tasks and demands on your time? Can you give me some examples?
49. Tell me about your experience presenting to groups. What has been your best and worst experience? Why?

8 Putting It All Together: Executing the Interview of Your Life

In this final chapter, we will briefly review what you have learned. More importantly, we will focus your efforts and provide a road map to success. It is never too soon to begin your preparations. I recommend you begin implementing what you have learned immediately.

Consider your preparation and the steps leading up to the initial interview. Review the interview model to fully understand how hiring managers are trained. The BBI model is designed to assess your past performance to determine whether you display the desired behaviors for a current position. Identify the desired skill set and competencies for a given position and work to tie your background to those competencies.

Practice with the sample questions to develop your catalog of story lines and answers. Practice and repetition are indispensable to building your confidence. As you progress, refine your preparation by tying your stories and answers to categories of questions. For any given category, you should have multiple answers to fit the question. This approach will better organize the catalog in your mind. Remember to apply the STAR format to all answers where practical.

Take time to research the company with which you are interviewing. The most valuable resource for this is the corporate website. Be familiar with the corporate structure, product line, pipeline, new products, and competition. Conduct some basic research on the industry. Be familiar with any major trends or issues.

In preparation for the phone interview, lay out your cheat sheets, questions, and key information on your desk. Spend adequate time in a quiet room collecting your thoughts prior to the call. The phone interview is designed to rule out candidates who lack the desired skill set. The blueprint for success in this phase is your enthusiasm, confidence, and ability to convey your strengths. One of the most important aspects of a phone interview is the close. Summarize why you are a strong candidate and get a commitment for a face-to-face interview.

Prepare and mail brag books to all members of the interview team. Your recruiter or HR contact for the company with which you are interviewing should be able to provide mailing addresses. You should schedule delivery of the books two to three days prior to your interviews.

At the opening of the face-to-face interview, inform the interviewer that you have some things you would like to share and ask her to save a few minutes for you at the end. If asked to "walk me through your resume," remember to sell yourself along the way. Ask clarifying questions to determine how much depth or time is preferred. During your preparation, plan for both a three- to five-minute overview and a full presentation from your resume. Begin at college and discuss the rationale for every move made. Reinforce your clarity of thought, deliberate decisions, and lessons learned with each change in your career. Remember to answer all appropriate questions in the STAR format. Take advantage of opportunities to use your brag book during the interview. If you have documentation in your book that supports your answer, open the book and share it with the interviewer.

When given the time at the conclusion of the interview, have a typed list of intelligent questions. Take a few minutes for questions and then move into your close. Remember, the close is one of the most important aspects of a successful interview. I have had many candidates who performed in a stellar manner throughout the interview, yet failed to close for the job at the conclusion. *Hiring managers expect candidates to close.* When candidates fail to close, their odds for success immediately drop significantly.

My recommendation, based on years of experience as an interviewer, is to simply take three to five minutes to review the highlights of your brag book. The last page in your brag book is your "Why Me" page. That sheet should contain bullet points summarizing why you are the best candidate for the job. After a review of your qualifications, you proceed with a line of questioning regarding the interviewer's assessment of your candidacy. For example, "Have you seen anything during this interview that concerns you? Is there any reason you would not send me to the next round of interviews?" After gaining the interviewer's assessment, you proceed. If he has concerns, you address the concerns. When all concerns have been addressed, you directly ask if you may proceed to the next step in the process.

Ensure that you follow up with everyone on the interview team immediately. There are many ways to do this. My feeling is that it is much more personal to send a short handwritten or typed thank-you note. If interviews are taking place in a company's corporate office, you can ask the secretary to distribute the thank-you notes at the conclusion of your interviews. If the interviews take place at a hotel, you can have the bellhop leave the thank-you notes in the interviewers' rooms. Probably the safest and simplest method is to overnight the thank-you notes to the interviewers' mailing addresses. Your thank-you note should summarize a few of the key points from the interview and reiterate why you are the best candidate for the job.

You are now well-versed in the BBI model. You understand how hiring managers are trained and how you can best prepare to sell yourself to them. Having this information is an excellent foundation, but the concrete steps you take to prepare for your interview are absolutely crucial. The time and effort you invest on the front end of your interview will be worth it when you land the job you are after. Good luck, and interview to succeed!

Reviewing Interview Basics

- Dress appropriately. For a professional interview, that means a suit and tie with polished shoes, for men. Women should wear a conservative skirt or suit.
- Confirm interview details in advance. Know the time and location of the interview. If feasible, visit the location in advance to ensure that you know exactly where you are going.
- Arrive at the interview address fifteen to twenty minutes early. Enter the interview address ten minutes early.
- Treat everyone you meet as if he or she is the one making the hiring decision. Be pleasant and courteous.
- When shaking hands, look the other person in the eye, smile, use a firm grip, and hold for two to three pumps.
- Remember, your appearance and behaviors are as important as your discussion. Don't slouch, shift repeatedly in your seat, tap your foot, shake your pen, or otherwise fidget and squirm.

- Don't chew gum during an interview.
- It is acceptable to have a bottle of water with a cap at an interview.
- Interviewers are trained to monitor body language. Maintain good eye contact throughout the process. Good eye contact demonstrates honesty, engagement, and interest in the conversation.
- Request a business card for follow-up at the conclusion of each interview.
- If you don't understand a question, ask for clarification or to have the question restated.
- Make notes immediately following each interview to facilitate follow-up.
- Don't make excuses for shortcomings. If they come up in the interview, acknowledge them, discuss the lessons learned or how you would do things differently, and then move on.
- Don't complain or make negative comments about previous managers or employers.
- Refrain from discussing salary and benefits until the offer phase of the process.
- Make certain your cell phone is off.
- Let your personality shine through. Developing rapport with the interviewer is important. Be pleasant and positive.
- Have a thoughtful list of questions typed and prepared for the hiring manager.
- Maintain your professionalism, even if the interviewer establishes a casual atmosphere. Remember, you are being evaluated.